The Client Perspective on Evaluation

Jeri Nowakowski, *Editor*
Northern Illinois University

NEW DIRECTIONS FOR PROGRAM EVALUATION

A Publication of the American Evaluation Association

*A joint organization of the Evaluation Research Society
and the Evaluation Network*

MARK W. LIPSEY, *Editor-in-Chief*
Claremont Graduate School

Number 36, Winter 1987

Paperback sourcebooks in
The Jossey-Bass Higher Education and
Social and Behavioral Sciences Series

Jossey-Bass Inc., Publishers
San Francisco • London

Jeri Nowakowski (ed.).
The Client Perspective on Evaluation.
New Directions for Program Evaluation, no. 36.
San Francisco: Jossey-Bass, 1987.

New Directions for Program Evaluation Series
A publication of the American Evaluation Association
Mark W. Lipsey, *Editor-in-Chief*

New Directions for Program Evaluation is published quarterly by
Jossey-Bass Inc., Publishers (publication number USPS 449-050),
and is sponsored by the American Evaluation Association.
Second-class postage rates are paid at San Francisco, California,
and at additional mailing offices. POSTMASTER: Send address
changes to Jossey-Bass Inc., Publishers, 433 California Street,
San Francisco, California 94104.

Editorial correspondence should be sent to the Editor-in-Chief,
Mark Lipsey, Psychology Department, Claremont Graduate School,
Claremont, Calif. 91711.

Library of Congress Catalog Card Number LC 85-644749

International Standard Serial Number ISSN 0164-7989

International Standard Book Number ISBN 1-55542-942-4

Cover art by WILLI BAUM

Manufactured in the United States of America

Ordering Information

The paperback sourcebooks listed below are published quarterly and can be ordered either by subscription or single copy.

Subscriptions cost $52.00 per year for institutions, agencies, and libraries. Individuals can subscribe at the special rate of $39.00 per year *if payment is by personal check*. (Note that the full rate of $52.00 applies if payment is by institutional check, even if the subscription is designated for an individual.) Standing orders are accepted.

Single copies are available at $12.95 when payment accompanies order. (California, New Jersey, New York, and Washington, D.C., residents please include appropriate sales tax.) For billed orders, cost per copy is $12.95 plus postage and handling.

Substantial discounts are offered to organizations and individuals wishing to purchase bulk quantities of Jossey-Bass sourcebooks. Please inquire.

Please note that these prices are for the academic year 1987–88 and are subject to change without prior notice. Also, some titles may be out of print and therefore not available for sale.

To ensure correct and prompt delivery, all orders must give either the *name of an individual* or an *official purchase order number*. Please submit your order as follows:

Subscriptions: specify series and year subscription is to begin.
Single Copies: specify sourcebook code (such as, PE1) and first two words of title.

Mail orders for United States and Possessions, Latin America, Canada, Japan, Australia, and New Zealand to:
Jossey-Bass Inc., Publishers
433 California Street
San Francisco, California 94104

Mail orders for all other parts of the world to:
Jossey-Bass Limited
28 Banner Street
London EC1Y 8QE

New Directions for Program Evaluation Series
Mark W. Lipsey, *Editor-in-Chief*

Contents

New Directions for Program Evaluation

A Quarterly Publication of the American Evaluation Association
(A Joint Organization of the Evaluation Research Society and the
Evaluation Network)

Editor-in-Chief:

Mark W. Lipsey, Psychology, Claremont Graduate School

Editorial Advisory Board:

Scarvia B. Anderson, Psychology, Georgia Institute of Technology
Gerald L. Barkdoll, U.S. Food and Drug Administration, Washington, D.C.
Robert F. Boruch, Psychology, Northwestern University
Timothy C. Brock, Psychology, Ohio State University
Donald T. Campbell, Social Relations, Lehigh University
Eleanor Chelimsky, U.S. General Accounting Office, Washington, D.C.
James A. Ciarlo, Mental Health Systems Evaluation, University of Denver
Ross F. Conner, Social Ecology, University of California, Irvine
William W. Cooley, Learning Research and Development Center, University of Pittsburgh
David S. Cordray, U.S. General Accounting Office, Washington, D.C.
Robert W. Covert, Evaluation Research Center, University of Virginia
Lois-Ellin Datta, U.S. General Accounting Office, Washington, D.C.
Barbara Gross Davis, Educational Development, University of California, Berkeley
Howard E. Freeman, Sociology, University of California, Los Angeles
Egon G. Guba, Education, Indiana University
Edward S. Halpern, AT&T Bell Laboratories, Naperville, Illinois
Harry P. Hatry, The Urban Institute, Washington, D.C.
Michael Hendricks, MH Associates, Washington, D.C.
Gary T. Henry, Joint Legislative Audit and Review Commission, Virginia
Dennis H. Holmes, Education, George Washington University
Ernest R. House, CIRCE, University of Illinois, Urbana-Champaign
Jeanette M. Jerrell, Cognos Associates, Los Altos, California
Karen E. Kirkhart, Social Work, Syracuse University
Henry M. Levin, Education, Stanford University
Richard J. Light, Government, Harvard University
Charles McClintock, Human Service Studies, Cornell University
William A. McConnell, San Francisco Community Mental Health Programs
Jeri Nowakowski, Leadership and Education Policy Studies, Northern Illinois University

American Evaluation Association, 9555 Persimmon Tree Road, Potomac, MD 20854

Editor's Notes

The final responsibility for evaluation use lies with clients. Evaluators can do much to optimize usability, but ultimately clients determine whether and how to use evaluation reports. A client may be a board of directors, an elected or appointed official, or an administrator. Such clients are influenced by key stakeholders and constituents to whom they feel responsible. Professional evaluation standards (Joint Committee, 1981; Rossi, 1982) direct evaluators to attend to all these layers of audiences.

This volume focuses on the principal or prominent client of an evaluation and on the interaction between that client and the evaluator. Whether the clients are boards or single managers, they are the decision makers whose needs drive the evaluation design. The following chapters show clearly that good clients are important to good evaluation. The savvy clients described in this volume made evaluations better and more useful.

What emerges in these chapters is awareness that client skills and roles are different from evaluation skills and roles. Not all good evaluators can make the transition to become good clients, as Michael Quinn Patton does in the chapter he coauthors with Marvin C. Alkin. Also, many clients expert in shaping and using evaluation do so without technical understanding of evaluation methodology.

Two overriding impressions strike one in these discussions. The first is that successful evaluation experiences are repeatedly described by clients as partnerships or team efforts. In each chapter, positive evaluation experiences reflect collaboration between evaluator and client, continual communications, and mutual trust in each partner's integrity. The second impression, and one ripe with lessons, is the importance of distinguishing role expectations for client and evaluator. In fact, team efforts appear to depend on an understanding of the differences in roles between the two. Conflict often stems from confusion or disagreement about who is responsible for what. Clarity of roles is important, and this volume attempts to contribute to that clarity, with particular sensitivity to the client's role from the client's own perspective.

Why Study the Client's Perspective?

Professional evaluators' concern with clients and their needs is not new. In fact, clients' concerns drive utilization-oriented evaluation, such as that characterized by the work of Michael Quinn Patton, as well as the emphasis on formative evaluation seen in many recent evaluation texts. Additionally, professional evaluation standards underline the importance of client-evaluator interaction. The Joint Committee standards (1981), negotiated with client groups, describe sound evaluation as having four characteristics: utility, feasibility, propriety, and accuracy. In a hierarchical arrangement, the most important quality of sound evaluation, utility, is significantly marked by clients' considerations. The presence of a client is what most clearly distinguishes hypothesis-driven research from decision-driven evaluation. Client's needs establish temporal and contextual boundaries, which in turn alter the expectations of what systematic inquiry can provide. Concern for clients is thus intrinsic to evaluation.

Still, while there is great interest in evaluation clients and stakeholders, precious little has been written about clients from the client's perspective. A noteworthy exception is Champion (1985). Some evaluation clients are better than others—easier to work with, more thoughtful about anticipating their needs, and more effective in putting evaluation to use. In this volume, we try to articulate some of the skills that make for good "clienting" in the eyes of clients and their evaluators.

There are several practical reasons for a volume devoted to clients' perspectives. One is to position the evaluation field to influence the market for evaluation services. Training more and better evaluators is important, but, correspondingly, there must be more and better consumers who value and can use evaluation services. The field of evaluation bears a large responsibility for educating clients about evaluation. When evaluation clients pass through our university courses and our training sessions and we attempt to teach them how to practice but not how to commission and use evaluation, we have missed an opportunity.

Many administrators are more likely to spend time as evaluation clients than as program evaluators. To that end, they need to know how and when to hire evaluation, how to influence its design and quality, how to negotiate reporting format and release, how to deal with controversial findings, and so forth. While teaching evaluation theory and process provides important knowledge about the field, it does not necessarily help students understand or master the client role. Students across a number of disciplines might be well served by more extensive training in the client's role of commissioning and managing internal and external evaluation efforts.

Finally, administrators and decision makers called upon at different times to play both roles—client and evaluator—must be able to distinguish between the roles and what is expected of each. It could be argued, for example, that administrators in state and federal agencies receive more criticism for failure to be good clients than good evaluators. Directors of funded programs are expected to evaluate outcomes, with little direction from state or federal clients as to purpose, key questions, likely impact, or key audiences. Recently, for example, when providing evaluation training for state special education staff, a director asked me how to deal with 350 thick, complete, and inherited evaluation reports from local districts. I would make the case that the very existence of such reports (and there are many similar sets across the country) signals a failure of client skills, not evaluation skills. With the growth of the evaluation field, it has become increasingly easy for educational and social agencies to hire evaluation consultants, but even a first-rate consultant cannot overcome a lack of client direction. Evaluation clients can and should be educated to promote utilization (see, for example, Alkin and Associates, 1985).

Overview of Chapters

Gunn provides, in the first half of Chapter One, a candid and sometimes humorous appraisal by a client of what can go wrong in contracted evaluation. Speaking from twenty-five years of experience, Gunn devotes the second half of his chapter to management strategies that keep a client on top of evaluation. While some of Gunn's warnings may make more than one evaluator uncomfortable, few will be surprised at the potential dilemmas he catalogues. Gunn's advice is for the "wily client," one aggressive in monitoring and controlling the evaluation enterprise. Many clients can learn specific evaluation management strategies from this chapter.

Chapter Two, by Marvin C. Alkin and Michael Quinn Patton, chronicles a large-scale evaluation of agricultural extension services in eight Caribbean countries. Several things make this chapter interesting and worth reading. The first is the interplay between two capable and experienced professionals, both of whom are knowledgeable about evaluation practice and use. Their reflective dialogue is particularly rich because they share a common set of values and concerns. Second, the chapter as a whole gives one a good sense of the politics, people, and planning behind an evaluation. Little was left to chance as these two pros constructed an evaluation plan that nicely dovetailed and enhanced the project director's work plan.

Joy J. Rogers, in Chapter Three, describes an emotionally charged reorganization of a school district in suburban Illinois. Her perspective, as president of the local school board, keys on the complex and value-laden school and community environment into which an evaluator was brought belatedly. With broad brushstrokes, Rogers tells a story that began long before the evaluator entered. It persists still. This perspective reminds us of the circumscribed and temporal roles evaluators play in a setting: Theirs is a brief appearance in a historical landscape within which other figures live and continue living. In fact, the stabilizing force that evaluators can bring to settings during periods of controversy and change is what Rogers thoughtfully describes and most values.

In Chapter Four, Penny A. Sebring and C. Dennis Carroll trace the client's influence on development of one of the most extensive longitudinal survey studies in the country. The negotiations between a reputable social science research center at the University of Chicago and the Longitudinal Studies Branch within the federal Center for Education Statistics serve as a working paradigm for others. Over the years, the actors in these negotiations have changed, and Sebring and Carroll prove to be trustworthy guides in reconstructing and analyzing the relationship between the two organizations. This chapter is rich in lessons about how clients and contractors negotiate surveys, how federal agencies promote contractor flexibility so as to facilitate timely policy analysis, and how the experienced contractor goes about securing relevant and reliable information for a client.

In Chapter Five, Jonathan Z. Shapiro and David L. Blackwell describe an evaluation in which traditional lines between client and evaluator are renegotiated. When Southeastern Louisiana University finds itself needing accountability data to justify funding, Shapiro is brought in to teach evaluation skills to project directors, collaborate in their evaluation designs, and take part in the collection and analysis of information. There are at least two important lessons to be learned here. First, it is clear that evaluators have a number of options in leveraging time and expertise. The result can be cost-effective and shared evaluation responsibility. Second, evaluation functions can be decoupled and creatively assigned, procedures we normally do not see in the conventional literature.

As internal institutional evaluators at the University of Illinois, Larry A. Braskamp, Dale C. Brandenburg, and John C. Ory in Chapter Six reflect upon ten important client criteria for evaluation. On the basis of long experience both in university and private sector settings, the authors tackle some sticky issues, including the sometimes untenable role of the internal evaluator, who is supposed to understand but not become part of management's inner circle. The chapter provides a sensible set of criteria proposed as critical to clients. Discussions that follow the criteria elaborate, without trying to resolve, the challenges for evaluators attempting to meet these clients' expectations.

In Chapter Seven, Thomas P. Faase and Steve Pujdak give readers a rare view of evaluation in a religious community. The issue addressed is the likely impact of a retrenchment that would greatly change the lives of many members of the community, drawing them away from work in other geographical sites. The questions for the client were whether such a sensitive issue could be treated adequately by evaluation research, and whether evaluation could provide useful information. Key to the answer is the selection of an evaluator schooled in the culture and values of the community. From the client's perspective, and from the evaluator's as well, the major lesson is that shared understanding of cultural setting between client and evaluator is requisite to success.

In the final chapter, Patricia F. First interviews Sally B. Pancrazio, chief of educational research and program evaluation, Illinois State Board of Education. Pancrazio is asked to consider her role as a client who commissions, contracts, and requests evaluation information from staff, outside consultants, and local school districts. She is candid about dealing with the "cautious researcher," who emphasizes statistical technique over utility and relevance. Pancrazio describes her steady effort over the past thirteen years to get more and better evaluation and research information for state policymaking. She concludes by anticipating both the growth of evaluation in her unit and a conscious push to use multiple information sources in addressing state policy questions.

Lessons Learned About the Client's Role

It has never been the intent of this volume to systematically study the client's role in each functional area of evaluation. Correspondingly, there is no desire here to force an artificial organization and clarity onto what, in many respects, is anecdotal and reflective information. However, it seemed somehow negligent not to bring together in these notes some of the cumulative and iterative lessons found within this set of chapters. Perhaps this brief summary will serve as a starting point for readers to think more deeply about clients—their roles, skills, and perspectives relative to evaluation practice.

Focusing Evaluation. The clients in these chapters play a key role in establishing the evaluation purposes and intended audiences. They lay out decisions that are to be made, issues that need to be addressed, and the timelines that must be met if the evaluation is to be useful. Clients let evaluators know who the stakeholders are and help anticipate audience needs. They forewarn evaluators of political pitfalls and collaborate in their avoidance. Through their understanding about the background and status of the evaluand, they help influence specific evaluation objectives, evaluation approach, and general reporting strategy. Experienced clients look for other opportunities to use the data being generated and try to see if other, less urgent questions might also be addressed.

Clients in these chapters typically are responsible for selecting credible evaluators or evaluation teams. Experienced clients know why they are hiring a particular evaluator and often structure evaluation teams to maximize credibility across a wide range of users. From the outset, these clients help establish and preserve the evaluator's credibility.

Design. While most clients in these chapters prefer that the specific and detailed design be handled by the evaluation consultant, they nontheless play an aggressive role in setting design parameters. For example, clients can determine what is to be measured or studied and generally how. They guide evaluators in selecting information sources and procedures that will be credible to stakeholders and to themselves.

Many clients also want to play a quality-assurance role in evaluation design. After influencing major design features, for example, they take on a review and revision role—okaying instruments, sampling procedures, consent forms, analysis plans, and so forth. Further, they influence evaluation implementation schedules, sometimes breaking evaluation into separate and discrete phases. Clients influence the kind of expertise to be brought in during phases of design implementation and often stipulate review boards and criteria for evaluating the design.

Clients often require and benefit from detailed planning at the design stage. They use written evaluation designs as statements of work about what the evaluation will do, what is to be delivered and when, and so forth. The evaluation design by request parallels and enhances a project work plan.

Information Collection. While evaluation consultants typically operate with much autonomy when collecting data, some clients put in-house staff in charge of overseeing the conduct of evaluation. Quality-control checkpoints are built in to review instruments, coding, data-cleaning procedures, and so forth. If raw data are to be released, clients influence organization, storage, and accessibility. Some clients bring in experts to audit the information-collection process and procedures for guaranteeing anonymity.

Most clients in this volume advocate for flexibility, negotiating with evaluators for more, different, and more timely information as their needs change. Experienced clients take front-end responsibility for establishing what constitutes credible information, although on more than one occasion in this volume the selected information base cannot serve all the client's stakeholders effectively.

Analysis. In most of these chapters, analysis of quantitative and qualitative data is the sole responsibility of the evaluator. In one case, analysis is decoupled from information collection and handled by personnel within the client agency or further subcontracted. Clients also influence criteria for interpretation of findings. However, analysis generally seems to be the area where clients most often defer to the technical expertise of consultants, and where consultants most steadfastly hold on to their authority.

Interpretation and reporting of findings extends and overlaps analysis. Most clients in these chapters negotiate aggressively for influence over what is reported, how, and when.

Management. Many tricks of the trade for managing evaluation are identified by clients. Internally, clients seek front-end commitment from their own staffs and colleagues for specific evaluation responsibilities. They estimate timelines and budgets for their own involvement. Some clients build in ad hoc or ongoing advisory committees to monitor evaluation implementation. At least one client requests that such a committee be built in to the consultant's proposal. Most clients request regular reports about the progress of an evaluation—for example, asking for monthly financial reports on long-range projects.

When selecting an evaluation consultant, many clients look at management as well as technical skills of contractors. Do they have staff with management experience, is there a sound fiscal control system, are they able to deal with political problems, do they have a track record of handling time crunches or budget problems well? Do they have a solid knowledge of constraints in the field? To select evaluators with solid management skills, clients review past products, experiences with other clients, and staff credentials.

Clients enhance evaluation by opening up internal organizational channels for evaluators, keeping them informed about important changes and generally facilitating their work. This is done in part through close interface between evaluation plan and project work plan. From the client's perspective, evaluation can help management, but only if evaluation is itself well managed.

Reporting. Clients can play a consequential role in guiding reporting, and experienced clients appear to know that. Many build in regular reporting to ensure that, first, they are never caught by surprise and, second, that they can optimize their chances for using information formatively. Most clients collaborate with evaluators in editing reports for audience needs. This collaboration may be formalized contractually but, most important, is based on mutual trust.

From the client's perspective, the best evaluation reports are brief, concise, understandable, and on time. Typically, clients want practical recommendations and action steps to be included. Many clients stipulate brief executive summaries, sustained by more technical reports, to be shared with key audiences.

To keep evaluation reports from being buried within an organization and to keep them sensitive to audience needs, many clients stipulate a broad review. Permission to publish also ensures release of evaluation information by the evaluator, if not by the client agency.

Summing Up

Evaluators come to evaluation with variable skills, backgrounds, assumptions, and philosophies. So do clients enter evaluation contracts with varying notions about how involved they should be, what outcomes

8

are reasonable to expect, and what good evaluation ought to look like. Some clients choose to be involved in the evaluation process throughout; others want minimal but timely involvement. In learning about clients, we must be careful not to make generalizations about style too quickly, as the chapters that follow will demonstrate.

While we hope this slim volume makes a contribution to understanding the client's perspective on evaluation, there are many areas yet to explore. For example, the emphasis here is on contracted external evaluation. We know that evaluation is a management tool sometimes handled by internal units within an organization. While the chapter by Braskamp, Brandenburg, and Ory includes problems encountered by internal evaluators, generally this volume focuses on hired, external, and ad hoc evaluations.

This has been an exploratory exercise. We hope our foray will yield substance for more and deeper study of the client's perspective and influence on evaluation. The intent has been to produce a readable volume, biased toward the client's perspective and sprinkled with some useful and new lessons. Last, and most important, we hope the volume brings a sideways glance at the evaluation landscape, permitting a new perspective on otherwise familiar territory.

Jeri Nowakowski
Editor

References

Alkin, M., and Associates. *A Guide for Evaluation Decision Makers.* Newbury Park, Calif.: Sage, 1985.

Champion, H. "One Public Manager's View of Program Evaluation." *Evaluation News,* 1985, *6* (1).

Joint Committee on Standards for Educational Evaluation. *Standards for Evaluations of Educational Programs, Projects, and Materials.* New York: McGraw-Hill, 1981.

Rossi, P. H. (ed.). *Standards for Evaluation Practice.* New Directions for Program Evaluation, no. 15. San Francisco: Jossey-Bass, 1982.

Jeri Nowakowski is assistant professor in the Leadership and Educational Policy Studies Department at Northern Illinois University. She is director of the College Office of Educational Evaluation and Policy Studies and is coauthor of several books, including Program Evaluation: A Practitioner's Guide for Trainers and Educators *and* A Handbook of Educational Variables. *She is past president of the Evaluation Network and has served as interim board president for the American Evaluation Association.*

The wily client knows what potential pitfalls to avoid in evaluation and has management strategies for keeping an evaluation on track.

Client Concerns and Strategies in Evaluation Studies

Walter J. Gunn

Clients who commission evaluation studies may be based in private industry, universities, or government. Even though these clients may differ in many ways, they do share many of the same concerns when it comes to initiating an evaluation study of an important program. To use the word *concerns* as I have here may be a gross understatement of what we clients actually experience. Introspectively, it would perhaps be better to say that we share the same *terrifying visions* whenever we contemplate having someone else evaluate one of our prized programs. This is not a vague and unwarranted general fear; it is definable and specific and has been learned through hard experience over the twenty-five years I have spent as a client in government, private industry, and academia.

What are some of the things that can go wrong with an evaluation, from the client's perspective, and what specific actions can wily clients take to make sure that some of these problems do not happen? When asking what kinds of things can go wrong with evaluations, I feel like the proverbial mosquito in a nudist colony; I hardly know where to begin, but I'll try. To start with, a client may commission an evaluation study that turns out to be well designed, carried out according to plan, accurately analyzed, and clearly described in a final report, only to have it totally rejected by the primary audience for whom it was intended.

J. Nowakowski (ed.). *The Client Perspective on Evaluation.*
New Directions for Program Evaluation, no. 36. San Francisco: Jossey-Bass, Winter 1987.

What has gone wrong? Perhaps the audience feels that the client has had too much influence over the results or that audience representatives should have been consulted about the design. Maybe the audience members did not understand some of the limitations imposed by reality during planning because they were not there to participate.

Worse yet, imagine a situation where, because of the client's desire to demonstrate that he could not possibly influence the results, he initiates an evaluation contract study over which he has no control at all. Now he is in real trouble. Any number of disasters may occur under these conditions. For instance, the evaluation contractor (hereafter simply called the *contractor*) may conduct a summative evaluation when perhaps the client really needs a formative study. The final report may turn out to be more appropriate to some audience other than the one the client has in mind. The evaluation design and the test instruments selected by the contractor may be inappropriate, invalid, or unreliable. The contractor may present the client with a final report insensitive to important political aspects of the situation and resulting in a furor. The contractor may even surprise the client by publishing all or part of the evaluation study on his own, with timing and particulars bringing embarrassment to the client. Perhaps a journal cancels its previous acceptance of the client's submission of study results because of premature and unauthorized release of some of the data by the contractor.

Another favorite nightmare, and the bane of clients, is unanticipated cost overrun. In this scenario, the contractor informs the client at the end of a cost-reimbursable contract that the whole project has actually cost considerably more to conduct than originally anticipated. This means that the client must put one of his pet projects on the back burner and filch the needed cash from its budget or else dig deep into some colleague's pocket to find the additional funds. Neither of these predicaments is pleasant.

Some clients must secure clearance from another organization, agency, or arm of government devoted to protecting the public from unnecessary reporting burdens. (For the life of me, I can never understand why the public needs to be protected from voluntary requests for information, but this is a fact of life with which one must learn to live.) In the spirit of parsimony, and so as not to single out any specific agency at a particular level of government, let us call this hypothetical clearance agency by the generic name *ORP* (Office of Respondent Protection), regardless of whether we are talking about federal, state, or local agents or another organization with clearance functions. There are a number of things that can go awry when one must secure clearance for evaluation questionnaires. For instance, sometimes ORP will decide information requested is unjustified and, after considerable time and large sums of money have been spent, the client's request for clearance is denied. In other cases, ORP may itself order a contract cancelled to save the client the trouble. Not infrequently, ORP will approve only parts of the questionnaire, leaving clients with incomplete data upon which to base their evaluations.

There are also client concerns related to internal politics. Occasionally people with more political power than the immediate client may want to bury the evaluation report if they do not like the results. After months or years of work, someone further up the line who has publication-approval authority decides to put the report in his or her desk, in the hope that its "biodegradability index" is sufficiently high that it will simply disappear someday without leaving any residue.

Another concern of clients has to do with the increasing legal complications of conducting evaluation research. (If you took all the lawyers currently engaged in litigation related to evaluation research and laid them end to end, it would probably be a very good thing!) What is happening more and more is that parties involved in litigation are exercising their rights under the Freedom of Information Act to obtain information collected by the government and its contractors. Entire data sets also have been subpoenaed by civil courts. Clients are concerned about the drain on their time and resources brought about by the "Catch-22" of needing to provide the public with information to which they are entitled by one law while simultaneously trying to protect the confidentiality of information or personal identifiers of respondents involved in the evaluation study, as required by another law. The client worries not only about the moral issues of confidentiality but also about the future of evaluation research: What if the public should begin to feel that it cannot count on clients to protect the potentially embarrassing information they collect?

A final and legitimate client worry is this: Occasionally a contractor wins a competitive contract partially as a result of the stellar cast of characters proposed to direct and perform the evaluation. Later on, some of the stars are assigned to other and perhaps more important galaxies, and the client winds up with a replacement who smiles broadly and announces, "Six months ago, I couldn't even spell *evaluator.*" You know the rest.

Now you know some of the concerns we clients have about commissioning a new evaluation study. Perhaps when I explain some of the techniques we use to prevent these problems, some of the mysteries surrounding our ritualistic evaluation-contract incantations will become more understandable.

Techniques and Strategies

Establishing the Purpose of the Evaluation Study. The first step is to agree on the specific purposes of the study. Is this going to be a summative evaluation, to be used in executive decision making about future funding? Is it to be a formative evaluation, for program improvement? Or (God forgive) is it being conducted for purely political purposes, as a demonstration study? This is also a very good time to identify the intended audience for the study, as this decision will influence the objectives, style, format, and technical level of the final report.

Assembling an In-House Staff to Manage the Project. Start by analyzing the project to determine just what specific types of in-house skills and expertise will be needed to oversee the design and conduct of the study. For sure, you will need the help of someone who is knowledgeable about the program to be evaluated. You will need a specialist who is skilled in questionnaire design, statistics, and survey design. You will also need an experienced "wand waver" who can provide you with a realistic estimated budget.

Estimate in advance the level of effort that will be required of each colleague, and secure a commitment from each individual so that he or she will come into the project with open eyes and will therefore have no ready-made excuse not to pitch in when it comes to such time-consuming and tedious undertakings as proposal reviews, advisory panel meetings, and review of various draft reports.

Specifying the Work to Be Done by the Evaluation Contractor. Let us assume, just as an example, that the evaluation study will be carried out by contract, and let us further assume, for illustrative reasons, that the program to be evaluated is intended to change the behavior of some specific group of people, the target group. The challenge is to write a contract in which contractor and consultants will develop and conduct an evaluation of the client's program, with enough contractor independence to ensure the credibility of the study and enough client control to ensure the contractor does not take off on some wild tangent. First, describe the background and purpose of the project to be evaluated. Next, explain why the evaluation is needed, and identify the audience for whom it is intended. Finally, prepare a clear contract statement of work (SOW) that describes exactly what the contractor will do, what will be delivered to the client, and when.

Specify in the SOW that a contractor's advisory panel (CAP) be named and convened early in the planning stages of the contract. Further specify that all candidates for the CAP must be approved in advance by the client. (There are good reasons for doing this.) Make it clear that the CAP will function in an advisory fashion, providing consultation on specific matters upon request, and will not take it upon itself to change the objectives of the study (this would require a contract modification). There is nothing worse than a runaway advisory committee that decides to do a different study than the one you had in mind.

It is important that the contractor employ a systematic decision-making strategy (such as a modified Delphi procedure) during CAP meetings in order to prevent more vociferous members from intimidating more docile (albeit knowledgeable) members into acquiescing without full discussion when important decisions are before the panel.

Require the contractor to chair all meetings, and be sure that someone is assigned to systematically record all the pearls of wisdom that fall from the lips of the highly knowledgeable (and highly paid) consultants. (Gurus, after all, are sensitive people, and they would be deeply offended if they thought for a moment that their advice was being ignored, even if they were being paid $500 to $1,000 a day.)

Specify the agenda for the first CAP meeting. Require the CAP to focus first on identifying the specific behaviors intended to be changed by the program being evaluated. Then have the CAP focus on identifying all the potential knowledge, attitudes, values, beliefs, and skills that could be expected to influence the likely appearance of each specific behavior previously identified as important. Have the panel identify the environmental, financial, material, sociological, and other factors that also could affect the likelihood of important behaviors or concerns. Then have the CAP attempt to agree on the relative importance of each of these factors, so that a prioritized list of specific objectives to be evaluated can be developed.

There is a reason why I like to start with the identification of important behaviors: I think that I have probably spent half my life sitting in CAP meetings listening to experts who endlessly discuss information and attitudes that eventually turn out to be totally unrelated to any behavior being measured. In self-defense, I developed this approach to help focus the discussions on related chains of measurable objectives. This approach, of course, is most appropriate for a formative evaluation, since it allows one to determine just where the problems lie when a behavior is not changed by the program, as was intended.

State in the contract that the contractor must use the prioritized list of important factors (described in measurable terms) to develop specifications for both the treatment (for example, curriculum specifications) and the evaluation instruments (for example, test specifications). This procedure, of course, assumes that the evaluation is being developed the way it should be: as an integral part of program planning. If you are not so fortunate and need to evaluate an existing program, then the list of factors can still be used to develop test specifications for the evaluation instruments. I believe that it is best to use criterion referenced tests (CRTs) if human behavior, attitudes, knowledge, skills, values, or beliefs are to be measured, since norm-referenced tests, which are best suited for comparisons of group data, are generally unsuitable for measuring individual achievement of the specific objectives needed for formative evaluations.

Specify that the contractor must determine the reliability and concurrent validity of proposed test items before using them in the actual evaluation. If validity is found to be low because of social desirability factors, then encourage the use of sophisticated measurement techniques, such as the random response technique, whenever they are appropriate and feasible.

Require the contractor, with the advice of the CAP, to prepare a detailed evaluation plan, including study design, test instruments, consent forms, analysis plans, and implementation schedules. Stipulate that client approval is required before the evaluation is actually implemented. This gives you one last chance to ensure that the contractor has not gone off on a tangent. Inform the contractor that there may be a delay of up to four months because of the requirement to have questionnaires and study plans approved both by ORP and by various and sundry review committees. The contractor should either plan to assign personnel to other projects during this review period or arrange for them to work on parts of the study not requiring such clearances.

Instruct the contractor to submit a draft final report and to be prepared for a four- to eight-week review by the client. Make it clear that client approval of the final report is required, so that the client will have the opportunity to ensure that no politically insensitive statements or other blunders will adversely affect the ultimate reception of the report by others. Previous and ongoing reviews should ensure agreement or understanding of cumulative findings by the client.

Require the contractor to provide bimonthly financial reports showing the funds spent to date, the funds that remain, and projected expenses to complete the project. In this way, the client is less likely to be surprised by the eventuality of an avoidable cost overrun.

Specifying the Types of Expertise Needed by the Contractor. One should analyze the contract statement of work to determine the types of skills needed by the contractor. The client may want the contractor to employ experienced evaluation specialists, experts on tests and measurement, psychologists, sociologists, political scientists, statisticians, survey specialists, and program-content specialists. The contract SOW should clearly state that the study will require, as a minimum, each type of expertise the client thinks will be needed. The contractor should also be required to identify individuals possessing such expertise, provide their current curriculum vitae in the project proposal, and state specifically the duties of each person who works on the project. Make sure that the vitae show not only the academic degrees of key personnel but, equally important, also their fields of study and any publications that further support their claims to expertise. (Do not be shy about verifying the credentials of proposed key personnel. I once checked out a proposed principal investigator who alleged himself to have a doctorate in a specific field. The best that I could get his university to admit was that they had given this impostor a bachelor's degree in a totally different field.) It should also be specified that any changes in key personnel must be approved in advance by the client, as a way of blocking the "bait and switch" tactics of some profit-oriented contractors (known affectionately in Washington, D.C., client circles as "beltway bandits" or "Potomac River robber barons").

Ensuring Acceptance of Evaluation Results

First, the client should identify individuals and organizations whose acceptance of the evaluation results is crucial. If some of these individuals work in the client's organization or agency, efforts should be made to involve them in the planning of the project, development of the contract statement of work, and proposal reviews. If possible, their participation should also be solicited as co-project officers, who will jointly monitor the progress and quality of the evaluation contract. If this is not possible, then they should be invited to serve as members of a special project-oversight committee, with less of a time commitment required. The main thing is to involve them in some way. The contractor should be required to invite representatives of various important organizations to serve on the CAP. The contractor also should be encouraged to invite well-regarded and powerful experts (the gurus) in specific technical areas either to serve on the CAP or to be special consultants. Since these are the people who normally would be inclined to comment on the project after the results are published, it is far better to have them involved and already possessed of a sense of ownership when that time comes. (I have yet to see any important evaluation that was not later attacked by almost everyone who was not involved in its original design.)

If some organizations either cannot or will not provide representatives to serve on the CAP, special efforts should be made to keep them involved (for example, routinely forwarding draft plans for their review and comment). The steps outlined here are important because people's acceptance of a specific evaluation plan sometimes requires an evolution in thinking, which is possible only if they have been exposed to all the issues, potential solutions, probable consequences, and limitations experienced by those who work steadily on the project. Moreover, if such individuals have made good suggestions that have been incorporated into the study design, they are likely to develop a sense of ownership. This, of course, tends to increase their acceptance of the final product.

Ways to Retain Control over the Project

First, and most important, the client must create a clear and concise SOW that describes specifically what the contractor must do in planning the evaluation with the help of the experts who serve on the CAP. There are two reasons for giving the contractor and the CAP responsibility for detailed planning. For one thing, if the client is fortunate enough to have selected an experienced contractor and an able panel, chances are good that they will provide a satisfactory evaluation plan. For another, such an arrangement helps to ensure that the project will have the credibility that derives from the relatively independent planning process I have described.

I also recommend that the contract should specify an evaluation project to be performed in several separate and distinct phases. At the end of each phase, the contractor must develop a detailed plan for conducting the next phase. Client approval of each phase must also be secured before any work may begin on the next one. This requirement gives the client a limited kind of de facto control, which may turn out to be important if some major mistake is about to be made. Such an arrangement periodically allows the client to check the contractor's plans for the next phase against the particulars of the SOW and provides the power and authority to put the project back on track if there is any tendency for it to stray from the original objectives. Having a copy of the contract with you at every CAP meeting can prove quite useful, just in case the gurus start getting really creative and try to change your study into a "goal-free evaluation" or scrap your valid measures of behavior for "behavioroids" or "behavioral vignettes," as has been tried on me at one time or another.

How to Ensure That Results Will Not Be Buried

Clients, like most other people, must function in a political environment, regardless of whether they work in government, private industry, or academia. It would be foolhardy to ignore the internal and external political realities that influence evaluation research, because to do so permits science to take a back seat to bureaucratic expediency. For example, a client may have reason to believe that someone in his or her own or some other organization has the power and the desire to bury the evaluation results. If the client feels that full disclosure is important, there are steps that can be taken early in the planning of the contract to prevent this unfortunate situation from ever occurring.

There are at least two main ways in which evaluation reports can be buried. In one scenario, an evil-minded reviewing official simply puts the report in his desk and fails to approve its dissemination or publication. In the other, the detractor convenes an ad hoc review committee of like-minded associates, with a predictable result: a negative review, with lots of vague criticisms and charges that the report is inadequate, off target, ill conceived, or of low quality.

There are several preventive steps that can be taken. The client can require in the original SOW that the contractor give the final report the widest possible circulation for review and comment (by important members of the intended target audience, evaluation experts, and program officials) before delivering it to the client. A favorable review of high-caliber experts and important others makes it very difficult for some bureaucrat to come up with a vague but scathing negative review of the final report in order to block its publication and dissemination. In such cases, the client should make sure that there is no "boilerplate clause" in the contract that could limit in any way the contractor's ability to publish the results in journals or make presentations of the data at professional meetings. Thus, the client could encourage the contractor to publish the data if there were any doubt about the intentions of others in regard to the disposition of the final report.

Sometimes, however, a client needs a contract clause that limits the contractor's ability to publish or otherwise release the study results— for example, when premature comments from the contractor would inhibit the client's ability to publish or disseminate the results in the way he or she would like.

Managing Clearance Problems

Before contracting for an evaluation, the client should try to determine whether personal information of a sensitive nature will be needed to complete the evaluation study. If such sensitive information is crucial to the success of the project, and if the client believes that it will be impossible to obtain official clearance to collect this information, then the SOW must allow the contractor to obtain the necessary information from other organizations that have independently collected it or that plan to do so. (I never cease to be amazed at how often contractors can buy such information from others.)

If sensitive information must be collected, and if there is no choice other than collecting it with the project's funds, then the client should request the contractor to prepare a solid justification of the need for each item and to provide endorsements from representatives of the target group, from experts in related technical fields, from church groups, or from any other organizations that might hold sway with ORP. Including some limited pretest results in the clearance request is also helpful if questions about response rates or validity are liable to be raised by ORP as objections to the types of questions to be asked. Securing ORP clearance for the study concept before soliciting proposals for the study does much to bolster the client's confidence in the eventual clearance of survey instruments and is highly recommended, if time permits.

Confidentiality

Whenever possible, data-collection instruments should be designed in such a way that respondents' names and other personal identifiers are not collected at all. If the study design absolutely requires the collection and retention of names and personal identifiers, even for a relatively short period of time, one should not automatically assume that it will be necessary to promise confidentiality to win respondents' cooperation. A pretest of the interview should be conducted first. If the response rate is acceptable, then a promise to protect the confidentiality of the data may not be necessary. Regardless of whether confidentiality has been promised, every effort should be made to protect the privacy of the respondents. One helpful technique in this regard is to remove respondents' names and personal identifiers from the survey instruments after the interview and replace them with code numbers designed to permit linkage with other relevant data that may be collected. The contractor retains the key that links codes with names just long enough to verify data and conduct any necessary follow-up. The key is then destroyed. Access to the data should be given only to employees and to consultants of the contractor, on a need-to-know basis.

Regardless of the precautions they take to minimize confidentiality problems, both the client and the contractor should be prepared to accept the significant and inevitable legal costs and staff time required to handle confidentiality issues. There is a great deal of uncertainty at this time about the right to information versus the right to privacy, and there will be many court tests before clients and contractors know exactly where they stand in such conflicts.

So there you have it: I have shared with you some of my concerns and some of my most cherished secrets for dealing with them, for two reasons. I hope to increase understanding between clients and evaluators and improve their ability to cooperate (sometimes like trying to mate porcupines). I also hope that clients who read this will find some of my suggestions helpful in planning their future evaluation studies.

Walter J. Gunn is president of Arlington Associates in Washington, D.C., a firm that provides consultation on evaluation and survey research. He has over twenty-five years of experience as a client of evaluation and has served as project officer for several national health-related evaluations.

A knowledgeable and experienced evaluator becomes the principal user of a design to make program evaluation and administration mutually reinforcing.

Working Both Sides of the Street

Marvin C. Alkin, Michael Quinn Patton

We want to tell a story, the still-evolving story of an evaluation process that has made a difference. It is also, in our minds, a relatively unusual example of evaluation use. In our experience, we do not have any corollaries to match the continuity and magnitude of this evaluation, in which continuous phases took on new questions as the project evolved.

One highlight of this case was the presence of a sophisticated user (Patton) who was familiar with the evaluation process and interested in its use. The literature (Alkin, Daillak, and White, 1979; Patton, 1986) points to the importance of the intended user's involvement as a factor in utilization. This instance is an almost classic example of participation by a knowledgeable and involved primary user. The evaluation team was also headed by a utilization-oriented evaluator (Alkin). Together, we would like to reflect on this story, partly in narrative and partly in a conversational format.

Context

The Project: The Caribbean Agricultural Extension Project (CAEP), funded by U.S. Aid to International Development (AID, the foreign-aid agency of the U.S. government).

The authors acknowledge with appreciation the careful reading and the excellent editorial and substantive suggestions provided by Jeri Nowakowski.

J. Nowakowski (ed.). *The Client Perspective on Evaluation.*
New Directions for Program Evaluation, no. 36. San Francisco: Jossey-Bass, Winter 1987.

Project Purpose: Increasing the effectiveness of agricultural extension services in eight Caribbean countries.

Key Stakeholders: (1) U.S. AID Caribbean office, especially the agricultural staff; (2) University of the West Indies Project staff and faculty in agriculture; (3) agriculture and extension officials in the eight participating countries; (4) farmers and their representatives on the project advisory committee; and (5) the American academic staff involved in the project, including Michael Quinn Patton as project director.

Evaluation Team: Marvin C. Alkin, UCLA, team leader; Jerry West, an agricultural economist at the University of Missouri, chosen by U.S. AID; Marlene Cuthbert, University of the West Indies (UWI) communications specialist, chosen by the UWI project staff; and Kay Adams, then of Ohio State University, chosen by the American academic participants. The evaluation team was carefully chosen for balance and credibility, to represent the various primary stakeholders; for disciplinary diversity; for gender balance; and for expertise in various project aspects (agriculture, communications, higher education, and vocational education).

Evaluation Scope: The CAEP evaluation covered a two-year period. It involved both data collection and the creation of a data-documentation system. Data were collected from eight Caribbean countries (Antigua, Belize, Dominica, Grenada, Montserrat, St. Kitts/Nevis, St. Lucia, and St. Vincent). In addition, data were collected at the primary training institution (University of West Indies, Trinidad) and at various other agencies in Trinidad and Barbados. Data collection involved interviews, review of documents (work plans, lists, and so on), and attendance at meetings. Detailed protocols guided all interviews, and data sheets were sent before visits to assist in preparations for document review. In addition, the evaluators conducted a set of case studies among farmers as evidence of program impact. The evaluation report had individual country summaries, as well as summaries by evaluation topic. The total evaluation cost for this $5 million project was $150,000.

Credibility of the Evaluation Team

Knowing that the credibility of the evaluation team would affect the evaluation's use, Patton, the project director, continuously stressed the competence of the team and the representativeness of its selection.

Alkin: The fact that you kept saying that this was a credible team seemed to add to the credibility. And over a period of time, we became credible because you told the other users that we were. We surely did have some initial credibility—but it was extended by your actions.

Patton: The basis of trustworthiness for each evaluation team member was different and contributed to overall team credibility. Marlene, a UWI faculty member, represented the Caribbean perspective and, in ideological terms, her perspective was necessary to make the whole process credible to UWI staff. Her presence was an assurance that the evaluation wasn't something that was being controlled by the outside, because she was an "inside" Caribbean person. That was important to the team makeup and its wider acceptability.

A: It was initially her trustworthiness as an individual who was part of the team that added to the credibility of the team. But, over time, it was the team—as a team—that added credibility. Marlene suffered the fate of most insiders with respect to credibility— namely, she hadn't come from far enough away to be a real expert. You were able to assign expert status more easily to team members from farther away—"Well, we looked around for someone to head the team who was known worldwide . . ." As outside "experts," we had a greater measure of evaluation team member credibility at the outset. Marlene had a measure of trustworthiness. Each of us built our credibility as individuals over time in our interactions; but more important, we built our credibility as a *team.*

P: Yes, the team's credibility eventually transcended to some extent individual trustworthiness, but never entirely. Jerry remained the central person for U.S. AID. Marlene's individual and personal contacts with Caribbean staff remained important throughout. I looked to you to deliver a timely, usable product, even if your team fell apart. So the team emerged as a credible unit, but the individuality of team members—and what each brought to the team—was never forgotten.

Credibility is only partially what you start with; it is also acquired through the conduct of the evaluation (Alkin, Daillak, and White, 1979). As the primary user, Patton structured the evaluation team to maximize initial credibility across a range of users. Initial credibility, however, does not necessarily ensure that an evaluation team's credibility will be sustained.

P: It wouldn't have been hard to foul up your credibility. The initial credibility wasn't high enough to carry the team through a poorly conducted evaluation process. And it would not have been hard to foul it up. For example, at the very beginning—the first regional advisory meeting of all the stakeholders—if the team had imposed obviously external criteria for the evaluation, there would have been some problems. That is, if you had come in with pre-dispositions about what to evaluate, based upon conceptions and understandings from "the literature" on what agricultural exten-

22

sion is supposed to do, there would have been problems. If you had spent your time feeling that you had to test out some kind of adult-learning model or institutional change model out of the literature, that would have been difficult. And you might have derived from such a model a bunch of variables identified as important to look at, and maybe some instrumentation. That would not have gone down well.

A: In short, if we had been viewed as a group trying to do research or validate theoretical hypotheses, that would not have been acceptable. Our focus on user issues enhanced our credibility.

Evaluation as a Focus for Project Implementation

The evaluators worked hard to focus the design on relevant criteria. What resulted was a detailed, user-driven evaluation design, which became at first, the basis of a project work plan and, later, an internal quarterly reporting system. In such fashion, the evaluation team never was viewed as gathering extraneous data.

A: Michael, if you hadn't pushed it, the internal quarterly work plan and reporting system might not have paralleled the evaluation design. We could have done some external studies of our own choosing, which the staff would have had less of a vested interest in, and the evaluation results might not have been so relevant or readily accepted at the end.

P: The staff's monthly meetings were structured around the evaluation elements. The project team met once a month, and what they did in those meetings was go through the elements of the work plan, which were those ten or eleven major outcome categories, and discuss what they'd done in each one of those. That was how they monitored what they were doing and organized a work plan for the next month. I put that together on a quarterly basis. U.S. AID got used to seeing that. Everybody got used to seeing that, and it became identified with what the project was, in contrast to the initial-project paper proposal.

A: In essence, our elaboration of the evaluation design from the project paper proposal provided the framework for systematically conducting the project. Project work plans and operations were focused on evaluation outcomes.

P: That's right. I think the other thing the evaluation design did was to open communication about project areas where the evaluation found problems. It was possible to key right in on what those problems were. We already had common categories. There was no arguing, for example, about whether or not such-and-such was really a goal of the project, whether or not the things that weren't going so well were things we were trying to do in the project. The *evaluation-derived work plan* made it clear what we were trying to do. We avoided what sometimes goes on when the project plan of work and the external evaluation are not harmonized. Everyone was organized around the work plan. The project was organized around it. There was no way of pretending otherwise, although one or two of the project participants tried to on occasion. It was so clear that the evaluation findings were relevant, that their concerns were short lived.

One important facet of the evaluation, then, was the extent to which the evaluation design focused the project. The evaluation design and questions, in essence, became the structure for project self-monitoring.

A: Did you, Michael, use the presence of the evaluation team as the goad for accomplishing that purpose? I can imagine you saying, "Well, these evaluators are going to be coming down our throats, looking at us on these things, and we really ought to protect ourselves and make sure that we're doing the right things. So wouldn't it make good sense for us to try to use these external evaluation dimensions to monitor and keep track of what the project is doing in our internal quarterly progress reports?"
P: There was a piece of that—that's what I primarily emphasized at the outset. Of course, the staff knew where those external evaluation elements came from, because they helped develop them. You, as evaluators, facilitated and formalized that process.

I also played on an additional theme, which was "The evaluators have really done the work for us. Our project plan wasn't very complete, and we needed to develop a work plan for U.S. AID. Since the evaluators have really identified the major elements of the project, why don't we just steal that and make it our work plan, and save ourselves a lot of work?" We had a meeting for three days, where we were figuring out what we ought to do for a work plan, and just decided that it was sensible to use the evaluation question areas to be our work plan. In that sense, the evaluation *process* influenced our practice as well as our conceptualization of our practice.
A: That's right. This was a clear instance of the impact of the evaluation process on the operations of a program.

Building Confidence in the Evaluation

It has been noted (Alkin, 1984) that maintaining a user relationship in this evaluation posed many difficulties to the evaluators because of the distance and the phones, the travel, and all the rest. The evaluators could not have the frequent hands-on, drop-in, talk-to-people kinds of relationships that would normally be employed to build rapport, mutual trust, and credibility.

> *A:* Given these constraints, one of the ways that the evaluators tried to build confidence in the evaluation was to make sure that all of the steps leading to the conduct of the evaluation were well defined sequentially and that a clear relationship between steps existed. Therefore, the evaluators produced a design document that laid out the questions, and a related chart which indicated the kinds of data for each question, and a key showing which questions and data elements were appropriately collected from which sources. The procedure was incredibly detailed and might have been viewed as overly burdensome for most evaluations. In this particular evaluation, however, the evaluators felt a need to make sure that a lot of those steps were visible, as a means of maintaining credibility. That is, there was a clear and well connected *sequence* of evaluation activities, from design, evaluation questions, data, and instruments. And the important stakeholders "bought into" the final results because the sequence was so clear, and they had reviewed and approved it at a number of junctures along the way.
>
> *P:* I think the evaluation plan was an important element in the evaluation's credibility. I want to distinguish here between *your* personal credibility and the credibility of the evaluation. You were incredibly well-organized, Marv, and your attention to detail was superb. Certainly this demonstrated your competence, but having that detailed design on paper gave the evaluation its own face validity as a high-quality, carefully thought-out piece of work. The staff didn't go through the final design document in that careful a detail, because they trusted that to me and basically knew what it contained from the drafts. I know that U.S. AID looked at it. But more important than the content was what it communicated. The evaluation design showed a high degree of organization and competence, which added to the team's credibility, but also added to the design's validity and integrity.
>
> It also communicated to me and to the staff that *we weren't going to have to worry about making the evaluation happen.* The evaluation was really quite important to us. We wanted to learn from the evaluation—and we knew it could greatly affect future funding. We didn't want to be in the position of righting an incompetent, poorly organized evaluation. I personally would have had to provide any missing elements to make up for poor organi-

zation, because of the importance of the evaluation and the time-lines. I think what often happens in other settings is that the administrator doesn't take on that role: If the evaluator fouls it up, it doesn't get done. I knew enough to know that the timelines were important, and the structure—the high degree of organiza-tion—also made things credible to AID. It reinforced the timelines. And it reinforced some of the motifs of the evaluation: multiple data sources, confirmation of different pieces, the high degree of organization. The design helped the evaluation stand on its own, quite apart from your personal competence.

Of course, Marv, I hired you for the evaluation because I knew you would deliver, that you have an eye for detail and a concern for utility. But the others didn't know that, for sure, until the design was in writing. Then you had credibility beyond my recommendation, which sure eased my mind, and the evaluation stood on its merits.

In essence, the team's design report showed U.S. AID what the data sources were going to be and gave a preview of the evaluation report's format and content. U.S. AID apparently did look at the design paper carefully. Next, before the field work, Alkin had a meeting with U.S. AID to discuss their impressions. All of this prepared the way for the evaluation's subsequent use.

The highly detailed design paper served somewhat the same func-tion that prolonged personal attention would have served in a local pro-gram evaluation. Patton's experience and involvement, together with this detailed document, facilitated the close evaluator-client relationship that normally is part of a good user-focused evaluation at the program level.

Approving the Evaluation Officially

Another quite important factor was that U.S. AID was supposed to approve the evaluation design in writing. Various AID staff got involved because, according to their procedures, they all had sign-off authority. In essence, they had to agree on and "buy into" the evaluation. Since AID held the power of final approval, the evaluation team's participation at the first regional advisory meeting was to design an evaluation. The design team was not necessarily going to implement the design. Thus, the design team had an opportunity to build credibility and trust prior to being selected as the evaluation team. The project staff and others on the advisory committee had a chance to meet the evaluators and approve the design before any commitment was made to hire the team to do the actual evaluation. We suspect that it is relatively rare to hire an evaluation design team and get approval from primary users, and only then hire the evalua-tors. Normally, a contract covers the whole process.

P: Oh, yes. It was necessary for me to contract with the evaluation team in "stages." I needed you to establish credibility directly with the various other potential users, so that they wouldn't feel that this was my setup. It's because of my role as primary user, which you've identified, that I couldn't push too hard, or I would have destroyed the credibility of the evaluators. This was particularly important with AID because they had recommended only one member of the evaluation team [Jerry]. He was their only protection, or guarantee of independent judgment. They were unprepared to approve the full evaluation. The costs were too great and the risks unknown. They weren't prepared to do that. It was easier to get them to approve the low-risk piece, which involved $5,000, to produce something that looked very good to them, and then to go to the next step and say, "Well, this has worked out well."

They got a good report back from the AID staff member who attended the RAECC [Regional Agricultural Extension Coordinating Committee] meeting. And I'm sure that whether Jerry West did or did not directly contact AID was irrelevant; his agreeing to the plan added a piece of credibility to it, that the teaming was working out. Certainly if it hadn't worked out, Jerry would have let them know. If he had had any concerns about you or the team or the process at the design stage, I think they expected he would let them know. The staging is what allowed AID to feel that they were maintaining some control over this process, which they were, and maintaining some control also co-opted them into having to take the thing more seriously, because they were approving it all the way along. One thing that most AID staff do is read agreements. The primary AID contact person on this project was particularly meticulous. He does look at papers that come in, and therefore he knew that he had approved this evaluation, and they take those approval responses seriously.

Involving the Caribbean

Thomas H. Henderson, head of the Department of Agricultural Extension at the University of the West Indies, was a key Caribbean stakeholder. The Caribbean Agricultural Extension Project was originally his vision, and his credibility in and knowledge of the islands was critical to project success.

P: Following U.S. AID approval of the evaluation, Marv, the next major interaction you had with one of the users was the meeting with Tom [Henderson] in New Orleans. This was also important because he needed to become more involved in the process. He had been leaving much of the evaluation arrangements up to me, so it was really important for him to get further involved in things, and New Orleans accomplished that.

That meeting ostensibly was held to present a report about the project to a scholarly society, but it served other purposes, too. There were other ways that Henderson's participation in that meeting increased his participation in the evaluation. That meeting laid out Henderson's clear control of access to all the people with whom the evaluators were going to talk. It also clearly established all that he would have to do to make sure that the team's site visits occurred properly and efficiently.

A: Tom's involvement in the New Orleans meeting was of significant importance with respect to future impact, because getting to know us in an informal way added to the credibility that each of the members of the evaluation team had as individuals—they were real people. The meeting established both personal credibility and set out more clearly the organizational channels that would be followed in the conduct of the evaluation. Most important, it set out more clearly to Tom that he was in control of the organization channels that would be used by the evaluation.

P: And I think it established his commitment to the evaluation. He saw its scope and knew the people whom you were going to be interviewing. I could see that he was developing a sense of commitment to the evaluation as he looked over the interview questions and made suggestions for a few changes. The process of reviewing the instrumentation with Tom helped increase the extent to which those were Tom's questions. He was getting excited about hearing what the ministers of agriculture were going to say about the project, what other agricultural officials and technicians were going to say to the evaluators as independent people. As he looked through the questions, I could see that he shared my interest in knowing what was going to happen. It would have been helpful if U.S. AID could have gone through that detailed process as well. It would have been even nicer if the entire regional advisory committee could have reviewed the instrument. The more people who can review it, the more ownership there is—it makes it their questions. Even though we sent it out to all of these other stakeholders to get their review, it was not as effective as if someone was there to hand-hold and take them through the details.

There's another aspect that was important about Tom knowing what was going to be asked and getting excited about it. It set up the utilization that would occur out of immediate feedback to our field staff. We were anxious to get evaluation answers in their informal, casual content, as soon as you gathered the data, while it was fresh and Tom was set up and prepared, as I was, to hear the answers to those questions and to begin acting on them right away. The evaluation information was of less immediate relevance to U.S. AID because the actions they were going to take were going to be more formal and global. Our staff use was going to be more detailed and immediate. So, given that not everybody can be involved, the key people who were going to have to act on immediate utilization were involved and were prepared to hear answers, because they knew what the questions were. There really was only about two to two and a half months' lag between reviewing the instrumention and getting the answers. The final instrument review was in April. We met in Antigua in June for debriefing. The utilization began right there. Tom started changing things right out of that meeting. I went from the debriefing to meet with our staff to review and act on evaluation findings.

A: The primary immediate users were really you and Tom [administrators of the project staff] and the key U.S. AID staff members. Later, U.S. AID made a major decision about refunding. Meanwhile, the staff made decisions about modifying and changing programs based upon the initial data that were presented. These decisions were made all along, so that the actual evaluation process had continual impact.

The Larger Stakeholder Process

The project had established the Regional Agricultural Extension Coordinating Committee (RAECC), composed of key agricultural officials, technicians, farmers, and institutional representatives from the participating countries.

RAECC's participation as an advisory group to the project was not as a primary user, but rather as a strong and interested constituency (a political stakeholder group, if you will). Thus, RAECC's participation in the process helped to convince U.S. AID (the funder) that the process should be taken seriously and the evaluation results used. U.S. AID would not want to ignore forty fairly influential people who, in a formal way, had endorsed the evaluation.

P: RAECC was specifically designed as a mechanism to help achieve impact with AID and specific countries, as well as to hold the project accountable to Caribbean concerns.

A: I really don't know the extent to which we impacted the individual countries through the evaluation process, although we probably did, because by asking the questions and having them assemble the data, we maybe made them think about these things. Aside from a few isolated cases and several anecdotal comments, we really don't have specific data on the impact of the evaluation on each of these countries.

P: I think your skillful organization of the whole thing helped make it timely for the project and the countries. The timeliness was great. We had RAECC set up six months in advance. We had to have your findings ready. The timelines did not deal with the money running out, but with the staging at AID. I don't know if I've ever said this to you before, but I knew well before I told anybody else that we did not have significant short-term funding problems. The timing was related to when I thought there would be significant personnel changes in Barbados [at U.S. AID] and when the longer term [next phase] funding decision would have to be made. We wanted that decision made by existing U.S. AID personnel who knew the project and had bought into the evaluation. Bringing somebody new in would have been a problem, and thus there was very real time constraint attached to the evaluation. AID works so slowly in its decision process that even with a November evaluation report, it took until March for a request to Washington for new funding approval.

Thus the timing, in terms of both AID and RAECC, was important. The evaluation team did an excellent job of observing and meeting timelines, which had been carefully negotiated and jointly established by the primary user (Patton) and the head of the evaluation team (Alkin).

Furthermore, the way in which the executive summary was written was helpful in facilitating use within a tight timeline. The evaluators' commitment to summarizing findings in two pages and to raising a set of particular questions very much helped. Moreover, "keying" the summary to the body of the report provided evidence that there were backup data to substantiate the summary. The utilization strategy called for endorsement by RAECC, but such a large advisory group could not deal with three hundred pages. AID was subsequently influenced by this broad country involvement and consideration. Had there been no executive summary, or if it had been long, overbearing, or unreadable, nothing would have happened at RAECC.

P: The fact that it was so succinct and readable was important. It could be used by RAECC in that format. There was no other format that would have been useful, and without their use, we would have lost leverage on AID as an important potential user.

A: That's really interesting, because it's hard to find real, concrete examples in the literature of the importance of the executive summary. Here is a significant example, because if we had either not written an executive summary or written some narrative-format executive summary that was ten pages long, which is not unusual, it would have been virtually unusable at that meeting.

P: It was the exactly correct format, given the time constraints and the intellectual constraints of that environment—that is, my very clear agenda to them to adopt/reject the report and/or make modifications. Their involvement and adoptions were part of the leverage that was brought to bear on AID. They basically adopted the findings and forwarded it to AID, proposing the continuation activities. There had to be something there that they could get a handle on in a three-hour discussion. And that meant two pages— easily read, but well substantiated by the body of the report. You did it exactly right.

We did not have them judge the report—for example, judge or approve the evaluation—but instead asked them to look at whether or not the overall findings fit with their own experiences.

A: It was, in effect, a personal validation of the evaluation findings in the executive summary.

P: And that's all that could have been accomplished with forty people in half a day. There was nothing else that could have been accomplished up there. And they got into it. Some of them got quite detailed about the recommendations and how things should be rephrased. I think there were some improvements in that, both in their feeling of involvement, their greater ownership of the executive summary, and the further clarity provided. The fact that it was to be transmitted to AID enhanced their motivation. And in fact, people in U.S. AID who didn't read the report saw the executive summary. We circulated it there, and the U.S. AID evaluation officer, in particular, felt very good about it, and he was showing it to all kinds of people. He was showing them the whole report, but what they could read and what he'd show them was the executive summary. And they saw all this documentation behind it.

A: That's right. Providing an indication of the sections of the report from which that summary is derived adds credibility, even though a great deal of the time people never read those sections.

P: Those efforts in the executive summary communicated a number of things to AID about the thoroughness of the project. That helped with the momentum of the process.

Final Reflections

A: Michael, we've reviewed some elements of this evaluation and how we worked together. In summary, what was it like for you, as a knowledgeable evaluator, to find yourself in the position of a program director hiring and working with an external evaluator?

P: I knew exactly what kind of evaluation process I wanted. I knew who the major stakeholders would be, and I knew the characteristics of the evaluation which would be important for a really useful evaluation. Given all that, I also needed an evaluator with sufficient experience, integrity, knowledge, and skill to handle working with me, given that I would have specific expectations about the quality of the evaluation we needed. And, of course, the evaluator would have to be utilization-focused and user-oriented. You fit all those criteria beautifully, Marv, so for me it was a tremendous pleasure to see the evaluation process work as it should work. In that respect, the evaluation helped me in program administration, and I hope I helped make it a better evaluation. In that sense, we both worked both sides of the street. The program evaluation and program administration were mutually reinforcing.

What about you? What was it like for you to work with a program director and primary user who is also, in others contexts, a knowledgeable and experienced evaluator?

A: Well, some have asked me whether it was threatening to have you as the primary user. The answer is no. I knew what you expected in an evaluation and felt that what I could do would be quite compatible with those expectations. In fact, I would say that it was reassuring to be working for you. I knew that you would be there to take actions that would enhance the potential use of the evaluation. As we both have noted, one of the most important factors in utilization is an informed potential user, interested and concerned about evaluation results. I couldn't have asked for anyone better.

On another dimension, I found the situation somewhat amusing. I had just written *A Guide for Evaluation Decision Makers* [1985], which was designed to teach decision makers [evaluation users] how to structure evaluations to get their evaluators to do more useful and potentially utilizable work. Here, I found myself in the situation of a primary user "working" me, as the evaluator, to produce a more usable evaluation—and he knew more tricks than I had taught in my book. I found myself thinking about what agendas you had when different requests were made. While administrators typically have agendas and are political, you know how evaluators operate and what they do—and you were now working the other side of the street.

References

Alkin, M. C. "Sustaining Credibility and Relevance: Practical Aspects of Evaluating CAEP." Paper presented at the annual meeting of the American Educational Research Association, New Orleans, La., April 1984.

32

Alkin, M. C. *A Guide for Evaluation Decision Makers.* Newbury Park, Calif.: Sage, 1985.

Alkin, M. C., Daillak, R., and White, P. *Using Evaluations: Does Evaluation Make a Difference?* Sage Library of Social Research, Vol. 76. Newbury Park, Calif.: Sage, 1979.

Patton, M. *Utilization-Focused Evaluation.* (2nd ed.) Newbury Park, Calif.: Sage, 1986.

Marvin C. Alkin is a professor in the Research Methods Division of the Graduate School of Education at the University of California, Los Angeles. He founded and directed for many years the Center for the Study of Evaluation. His recent work has been on evaluation utilization.

Michael Quinn Patton is international programs specialist at the University of Minnesota. He is the author of several books on evaluation, including Utilization-Focused Evaluation *(2nd ed., 1986) and* Practical Evaluation *(1983), and has lived and worked in Africa, South America, the Caribbean, and Europe.*

Clients value the stabilizing force that evaluation can bring to settings troubled by conflicting value perspectives.

Using Evaluation in Controversial Settings: The Client's Perspective

Joy J. Rogers

This chapter describes the events leading up to an external evaluation in a small school district. The major focus is on the community unrest and the general level of tension, which shaped the evaluation contract, the reporting strategy, and the final use of the recommendations. I am writing from my former perspective as, first, a school board member and, second, the school board president during the life of the evaluation. The evaluator was a professor from a nearby university with experience in school district evaluation. The evaluation ran approximately seven months, at a cost of about $6,000. This chapter provides the client's perspective on the usefulness of evaluation in a controversial change process.

Our school district is of a type ubiquitous in Illinois but uncommon elsewhere. It is a small district (2,200 students), serving kindergarten through the eighth grade in parts of four different villages in suburban Chicago. We operate four elementary buildings and one middle school (for grades six through eight). The smallness of the district and its service to young children tend to make it very accessible to citizens. Thus, the level of citizen interest in our decisions tends to be very high. However,

J. Nowakowski (ed.). *The Client Perspective on Evaluation.*
New Directions for Program Evaluation, no. 36. San Francisco: Jossey-Bass, Winter 1987.

the small size of the district and its largely residential tax base forces us into fiscally conservative positions. Such districts as ours tend to operate with small central office staffs and of course tend to hesitate in hiring outside consultants. Districts like ours call in experts only when the situation is out of control and desperate. Although there is wisdom in hiring an evaluator to study needs and strengths before an educational innovation is implemented, this kind of social and economic climate, and the comparative insulation of small school districts like ours, are such that the district is unlikely to do so.

The innovation for which we ultimately hired an outside evaluator was a reconfiguration we call *paired schools*. This district reorganization resulted from a period of declining birthrates, combined with the already completed development of most of the potential housing sites within district boundaries, factors that caused our enrollment to drop from a peak of 3,800 to 2,200 students. This drop first resulted in a very unpopular decision to close three of our original seven elementary buildings (two in 1979 and the third in 1982). One of the factors taken into consideration by the board of education at that time was its commitment to operate one elementary building in each of four villages. This commitment produced some calming effect, because people's sense of village identity tends to be high in this area. Unfortunately, it also invited future problems, because the villages had differing rates of census change and quite different socioeconomic characteristics.

In the fall of 1984, only four years after the major school closings, the superintendent again found it necessary to notify the board that some attention would have to be given to the closing of a school, the redrawing of attendance boundaries, or the restructuring of attendance centers. The number of children attending one school was so low that instructional flexibility was lacking, while the number of children assigned to another school was so large that space in the building constrained programming. Inequities in class size between the buildings were inevitable, and numerous split-grade classes had to be offered. These split-grade classes were unpopular with most teachers and parents.

Facing these constraints, the board did not consider hiring an outside evaluator to help with the decision but did, however, hold a series of public discussions. The reconfiguration issue seemed (at least to board members) to have been competently, thoroughly, and accurately covered by the local press. Attendance at these public sessions was low. With the exception of local newspaper reporters and a few staff members who regularly attend board meetings, perhaps only half a dozen community members attended these sessions. Initially at these meetings we attempted to agree on boundary changes between the affected schools, but it became clear that we would be unable to do so because any proposed changes were likely to be viable only for a year or two. Several board members felt that only a longer-range solution would provide a stable learning and teaching environment. No one on the board wished to discuss the closing of yet another school. Although we had appropriate facilities to operate the district program in three of our four elementary buildings, the oldest and smallest school building, which had the smallest student population and the highest proportion of children who were transported by the bus, was the logical one for us to close, but it was in the most affluent village. That village had politically active and vocal community members. Five of the seven board members were also residents of that village.

An alternative was suggested by the superintendent: to pair our buildings into two sets of two buildings. One building of each pair could be operated as a primary-grade building, and the other could be operated as an intermediate-grade building. This alternative would equalize enrollments across buildings, provide large enough populations in each building to permit program flexibility, allow us to keep the current four buildings in operation, and provide enrollment boundaries likely to remain stable for many years. It sounded good, and we still did not think we needed an outside evaluation.

The Context and the Controversy

The public meetings continued into the early spring of 1985, and a majority of board members gradually became persuaded that the paired-schools model was the best one for the district. Because of the logistical arrangements that were required, a reorganization had to be made by March. As the reorganization decision became imminent, public attendance at board meetings swelled to the point where meetings had to be held in a gymnasium, with communication through a public address system. Thousands of signatures appeared on petitions begging us not to adopt paired schools. An activist group, Parents for Family Schools, was formed to try to prevent the school reorganization. Copious letters to the editor appeared in the local newspapers, opposing the paired-schools model. Still, on March 19, 1985, the school board voted by a five to two majority to adopt the paired-schools model. Even at this point, we did not realize that we could use an outside evaluator, as well as a study of options and likely outcomes.

The Decision to Hire an Evaluator

Informal conversations among board members began to anticipate the November 1985 election. Earlier, several board members had believed that once the decision was made public, concern would die down, and the decision would not affect the forthcoming election. Public interest remained high, however. The crowds at board meetings continued to force the use of the gymnasium and the public address system. These were obvious but unavoidable contributors to a confrontational climate. Tempers on all sides flared, and meetings now included exchanges of barely disguised insults between board members and the audience. Several speakers were moved to tears as they addressed us. Board members were accused of nefarious motives. The board members who had voted for paired schools happened to live in the most affluent village, and this fact was thrown accusingly at the board as a motive for the action. Unhappy parents claimed that these board members had acted only to preserve the school in their own village. Other angry parents, some of whom lived in that same village, accused the board members of caving in to the superintendent's wishes. Parents for Family Schools remained active and slated candidates for the fall elections. There was strong community pressure to elect a more responsive board that would communicate more effectively. A growing contingent of parents wanted a new board, which would reverse the paired-schools decision immediately after the November election, an action that would relocate two-thirds of the students and teachers in the district twice within three months.

We faced an alarming amount of disruption and confusion. Even the two board members who had voted against the paired-schools decision were desperate to avoid the potential chaos. This was the climate in the summer of 1985. It was in this climate that the board decided it needed an outside evaluator.

Our initial contract with the outside evaluator was made by the board as it was constituted when the paired-schools vote was taken. For the sake of convenience, that group will be called the *old board*. The old board was dominated by persons who favored the paired-schools option and who saw the evaluator as a tool for validating the paired-schools decision. It primarily sought a formative evaluation that would include information about how to make the paired schools even better. It contracted with the evaluator to provide that information over a year-long period. Of course, at that time, the board members and the evaluator were all well aware that the November election could change the climate under which the evaluation occurred, and everyone wisely agreed to draw up a contract that could be revised or terminated on the basis of possible changes in board composition. The evaluator was dealing with a client who could drastically change personalities and priorities after the election.

Negotiating Evaluation with a Changing Board Membership

The election did bring significant changes in the board's composition. Of five members up for re-election, only the two who voted against the paired schools were voted in. The other three seats on this new board were won by persons slated by Parents for Family Schools. The climate was foreboding, and the contract with the evaluator was renegotiated. The independence and the professionalism of the evaluator, as she sensed and understood the changed needs of the board, quickly won the confidence of all parties. She proposed modifying the original agreement, to obtain summative assessments about the efficacy of paired schools in addition to formative information for improvement. The change was agreeable to all parties, and the contract was modified. The evaluation design focused on four questions regarding the effectiveness of the new configuration: It proposed studying ten target areas in the district (including special education, media use, and teacher sharing) and producing multiple kinds of information to address each question. Techniques would include parent surveys, teacher surveys, on-site observation, interviews, and study of district transportation records and test scores.

The importance of the evaluator's role at this point cannot be overstated. She was the "glue" that held the school organization together. The mix of new and old board members, and a still-seething community, otherwise might have tipped the balance toward a second and midyear school reorganization. The fragility of the situation was compounded when a pro-paired schools member had to be replaced because of a job transfer.

Buying Time and Stability Through Evaluation

The presence of the external evaluator, and our commitment to a seven-month study, gave us stability and incentive to wait for outcomes of the evaluation. A useful feature of the evaluation contract was that the evaluator presented us with regular progress reports whenever new data became available. For example, in December an 80 percent response rate from a teacher survey indicated that most staff were pleased with the changes resulting from reorganization. The character of those progress reports—frank about reporting critical responses to various administrative and board actions—convinced us of the evaluator's independence.

Any evaluation, of course, takes place against a background of time. As the 1985–86 school year progressed and the November 1985 election was left behind, some things happened naturally. Families of kindergartners and families moving into the school district had never known the previous form of school organization. They tended to be pleased with the instruction their children were receiving. Parents with initial fears about paired schools generally found that the problems they had anticipated were not occurring. Their children were not isolated and without friends. The buses did not have accidents. The academic standards were not lowered. Property values did not go down. Also, their sense of having lost "their" school healed as a sense of identity was established with the new school. Some came to value the more diverse social contacts available to their children, as well as the broader range of experiences that the schools were able to offer, with more children, more teachers, and more heterogeneous groupings at each grade level. It also became clear that most parents were satisfied with their children's education, school, and teachers, even if they were unhappy about the district's reorganization. The evaluation reports tracked all these changes.

Thus, as the evaluator collected parent and teacher survey data in December 1985 and again the following May, the data were different because the situation was different. Throughout that time, the views of board members also were changing. The board, actively consulting the community through the independent evaluator, was discovering that the community was changing its views. One by one, board members came to support maintenance of the paired-schools organization on that basis. As the evaluator recognized that this was happening, she shifted the major focus of the evaluation back from the summative to the formative level. Problems that emerged in the new organization were addressed immediately by the board and the administration so that the students would not suffer. The evaluation made this possible.

Evaluator as Teacher

During these shifts in the board's focus, the evaluator also was very useful as a teacher. Without jeopardizing her own values, she often was able to ask questions that broadened the viewpoints of the various members. For example, when one board member wanted parents to identify their village of residence, the evaluator asked how that information might be used, speculating on what decisions it could create for board members. As already mentioned, the four villages in the district do vary substantially in socioeconomic status. Knowing the village of residence of respondents who expressed particular viewpoints would bring new information and offer more difficulties to board members who did not want to act for or against the wishes of only one segment. Using a structured series of questions addressed to this board member, the evaluator was able to help her see that she might not want this input. The information, while easy enough to get, would have been extremely difficult for this board either to use or to ignore.

Another unexpected benefit of the evaluator's presence occurred in May 1986, when the evaluator was conducting staff interviews in groups. One group, the special-education teachers, vigorously expressed concerns that the paired-schools model had made it difficult for them to obtain and serve special-education students in resource programs. Unraveling the complaints revealed that grouping children into schools according to the narrower grade ranges resulted in too few being available at the same times for special-education programming. Although the failure of the teachers to communicate this problem through organizational channels earlier in the year remained unexplained, the immediate response of the evaluator allowed the administration access to the information it needed to correct the problem.

The evaluator presented a final report to the board in June 1986. The half-dozen recommendations she made were now almost exclusively of a formative nature and embodied precisely the kinds of information board members felt ready to receive.

Evaluation Utility and a Changing Client

In reflecting on all that happened through the evaluation process, I have struggled with the interpersonal dynamics between evaluator and board and their implications for the evaluation process. Reflection on our behavior as "the client" reveals logical behavior with simple and comprehensible motives. Of course, those motives are collective motives because the school board is not one person, but seven persons who must act collectively or not at all. In acting collectively, the majority dictates the board's actions and the shift of a single vote can quickly modify, or eliminate, the relationship with the evaluator altogether. We were difficult as clients in that we were actually four different clients with four different sets of motives. First, there was the old board as a collective personality. It approached the evaluator with a need for public relations material to substantiate its decision. Second, there was the new board as a collective personality. It approached the evaluator with a need to fulfill the campaign promises of most of its members: to make decisions after considering community input. Third, there was a "neo-new" board. This is the group that the new board became as feedback showed that the community had come to like the paired-schools arrangement. Fourth, there was the administration. Although hired by the board, the evaluator had to work directly with the administration. Administrative motives would never be isomorphic with those of the larger and more transient board. The configurations represent four different clients. Although in retrospect they can be considered as distinct from one another, the problem of the evaluator was to sort them out in real time as changes were occurring.

Despite the unique structural aspects of our school district, finding such different and shifting personalities is probably common in work with any school district (and perhaps even city councils and state legislatures) over a period long enough for elections and membership shifts to occur. The evaluator in a transient consulting relationship must establish a relationship with the collective client that is sufficiently supportive and flexible to accommodate the inevitable changes within the client. First, it is difficult for the evaluator always to know which personality he or she is addressing. Second, the evaluator needs to identify the most viable collective personality among the several and help it to become dominant. Third, the collective client sometimes shifts to a less amenable personality and the evaluator may feel inappropriately discouraged or ineffective. Finally, the dominant personality that emerges after a successful consultation may not be the one most likely to thank the evaluator or provide a particular source of pride in accomplishment to the evaluator.

If attention to the interpersonal dynamics between the evaluator and the collective client can offer useful guidance, it is perhaps that the outcomes that provide a sense of job satisfaction and accomplishment to an evaluator may not be particularly important to a client, nor may the client be likely to provide them to the evaluator, even when the evaluation is successful for the client.

The evaluation we obtained was certainly successful in several important ways. It helped us avoid any further upheaval, improve our program, and become more sophisticated users of data. We may not have been terribly gratifying as clients. We did not do much to actively implement some of the evaluator's final recommendations. Major recommendations validated action we knew had to be taken. Some recommendations urged a tracking system to monitor and fix trouble spots. However, for example, ultimately we did not use the evaluator's work as a baseline to set up an ongoing evaluation system (one of her recommendations). In the future, we still may be unlikely to use an evaluator any earlier than we did before. Although the benefits of this evaluation were clear to those of us who remained through the change process, broad factors of climate are more enduring than the identities of the particular persons on an elected board who participate in any major change. A year after the evaluation, only one of the three newly elected board members remains on the board. The superintendent is contemplating retirement, and a large number of parents who responded to our last board survey said they were tired of being surveyed.

Joy J. Rogers is an associate professor of counseling and educational psychology at Loyola University of Chicago. She has been a member of the Matteson District 162 elementary district school board since 1984.

For a large, multipurpose longitudinal study, the Center for Education Statistics seeks a contractor who has the technical and managerial skills and trained personnel needed for nationwide surveys.

Contracting for High School and Beyond

Penny A. Sebring, C. Dennis Carroll

For this chapter, we intended to trace the role of the client through the design, conduct, and analysis of one of the Department of Education's largest surveys, High School and Beyond (HS&B). We soon discovered however, that because the conduct of a large-scale longitudinal study requires a close working relationship between client and contractor over a relatively long period of time, we could not limit our discussion to the client's perspective alone. Consequently, much of the discussion centers on the nature of the client-contractor relationship, as it has evolved and changed over time, and offers a combined perspective of roles and responsibilities, with specific reference to areas where the two points of view are not in alignment.

Planning and conducting the surveys involves a large cast of characters on the part of both the client and the contractor. We are just two of those actors, who have taken a step back to assess the respective roles of our separate organizations. While this chapter focuses on the client-

The authors wrote this chapter in their private capacities. No official support or endorsement by NORC or by the U.S. Department of Education is intended or should be inferred.

J. Nowakowski (ed.). *The Client Perspective on Evaluation.*
New Directions for Program Evaluation, no. 36. San Francisco: Jossey-Bass, Winter 1987.

contractor relationship in developing a particular large-scale survey, in studies like ours there may be general lessons to be learned about the nature of the client's role, the amount of control and direction the client possesses, and the legitimate areas where responsibilities can be negotiated and renegotiated between the two parties.

Scope and Nature of the Survey

High School and Beyond is a longitudinal study of the high school sophomores and seniors of 1980. It began in 1980 with a survey of approximately 28,000 seniors and 30,000 sophomores who attended over 1,000 schools. At that time, students completed a battery of tests and a questionnaire covering family background, school experiences, and future plans. Follow-up surveys have been undertaken in 1982, 1984, and 1986 on a subsample of about 12,000 seniors and 15,000 sophomores. In addition, the Center for Education Statistics (formerly the National Center for Education Statistics) has sponsored archival studies to collect high school transcripts, postsecondary school transcripts, and financial aid records for the elder cohort. NORC (National Opinion Research Center), a social science research center at the University of Chicago, has conducted the base year survey and all the follow-up surveys.

High School and Beyond is among the largest of the Department of Education's studies, in terms of both cost and number of respondents. The cost of each follow-up survey is currently running about $4 million, with money being spent over a period of three and one-half years.

The purpose of HS&B is to provide information on the characteristics, achievements, and plans of high school students, their progress through high school, and the transitions they make from high school to adult roles. Because of the breadth of the survey's coverage, data can be used to examine such issues as school effects, bilingual education, dropouts, vocational education, academic growth, access to postsecondary education, student financial aid, and life goals.

Data have been used recently, for instance, in relation to a policy debate concerning new regulations for bilingual education. HS&B data were employed extensively to examine home language and intensity of exposure to bilingual services and their effects on verbal achievement. It is interesting to note that groups both in favor of and opposed to bilingual education chose to analyze HS&B data to model the effects of various changes in the regulations.

The current secretary of education, William J. Bennett, regularly speaks out on the problems of education today and the programs funded by the U.S. Department of Education. In numerous instances, HS&B data have been the source of his remarks. The secretary has cited data from HS&B in his speeches about prayer in the schools, used findings on

the dropout rates for unwed mothers to focus attention on state assistance programs, and questioned the shift in life goals and aspirations observed in the 1972 and 1980 studies. He has also discussed the disparity between the HS&B reports of course taking and the guidelines suggested by the National Commission on Excellence in Education, and he recently questioned the rates at which colleges and universities are raising tuition and other costs in response to increases in student financial assistance.

The Client and the Client's Clients

The main sponsor of HS&B is the Longitudinal Studies Branch (LSB) of the Center for Education Statistics, Office of Educational Research and Improvement, U.S. Department of Education. LSB has the responsibility for designing and commissioning all longitudinal studies, including High School and Beyond.

When HS&B was first conceptualized, officials in the Department of Education made a conscious decision to design a multipurpose longitudinal survey that would furnish policy-relevant information in a number of substantive areas. Their intent was to launch a well-planned, coordinated survey that would eliminate the need for separate offices in the department to mount costly surveys of their own. The data could therefore be acquired at a lower overall unit cost and with less burden to respondents.

The Longitudinal Studies Branch is responsible for much of the negotiation and coordination involved in determining the parameters of the survey. Specifically, LSB has three roles in the department: to undertake the planning and development of requests for proposals (RFPs) for the major longitudinal studies, to monitor data collections, and to analyze the results.

While LSB is the principal sponsor, it clearly has a group of its own clients, whose information needs it is trying to meet. The foremost clients are the secretary of education and officials or line officers in the Department of Education: the undersecretary of education, the director of Program and Evaluation Services, and the Office of Planning, Budget, and Evaluation. Other less salient but important clients in the Department of Education are the Office of Bilingual Education and Minority Language Affairs, the Office of Special Education and Rehabilitation Services, the Office for Civil Rights, and the Office of Postsecondary Education. In addition, LSB eventually makes the data available to the National Science Foundation, the Government Accounting Office, the Department of Defense, the Congressional Research Service, and the Congressional Budget Office. LSB responds to specific questions from congressional staff and distributes tapes to about three hundred researchers at universities and research organizations around the country.

Survey Design

Survey design is a shared responsibility of LSB and its contractor. The process begins two to three years before data collection is anticipated. LSB staff, sometimes accompanied by NORC representatives, visit various education offices to explain and discuss the survey and the opportunities it affords for policy research. They also listen to policy concerns that each office may have, which could be answered by longitudinal data. During this time, position papers are circulated and reviewed. Comments are also sought from Department of Education offices, other agencies outside the department, scholars who are likely users of the data, and data-collection contractors.

When the RFP is drafted, it is also reviewed by the same groups who responded to position papers. NORC, in addition to other contractors who are potential bidders, evaluates past designs and provides original ideas for the RFP. During the bidding process itself, design features are further refined, with the winning contractor and LSB establishing the final design parameters.

In the base year of HS&B, design activities were continued as part of contract responsibilities. NORC carried out a full-fledged study of the policy questions that HS&B could address (Coleman and others, 1979). Later contracts also contained design activities for planning the next survey wave.

The final survey design very much reflects a compromise, which LSB has fashioned between its clients on the one hand, and the methodological and practical considerations involved in mounting the survey, on the other. The sample for HS&B, for instance, contains a higher percentage of Hispanics than is found in the population as a whole and allows reliable population estimates for Cubans, Puerto Ricans, and Mexican-Americans. This feature came about because the Office of Bilingual Education and Minority Language Affairs contributed funds to the survey so that it could obtain national data on Hispanic students. Oversampling has also been used to collect data concerning private schools, college access and choice, and high school dropout rates.

The content of questionnaires is also negotiated across groups. The Department of Defense, for example, has supported survey items related to career/military service decision making. The Office of Planning, Budget, and Evaluation has displayed a continuing interest in academic discipline items and in participation in such programs as special education, bilingual education, vocational education, and education for the gifted and talented.

The Client's Expectations of the Contractor

LSB looks for a contractor who possesses the technical and managerial skills, including those that concern fiscal control systems, to implement the specifications outlined in the RFP. The contractor must be able to manage numerous complex tasks. The sample must be drawn in such a way that oversampling of policy-relevant groups is accomplished while accurate estimates for the population as a whole are maintained. Numerous questions raised by various agencies in the Department of Education must be developed, refined, and streamlined to produce a clear, coherent questionnaire. Because the follow-up surveys rely mostly on self-administered questionnaires, the instructions and the layout must be unambiguous and easily understood by respondents at all educational levels, including high school dropouts.

In reviewing proposals, LSB considers both the corporate experience of the contractor and the credentials of its staff. The experience of a prospective contractor is frequently judged on the basis of the candidate's identification of field problems in the proposal and the alternatives he or she offers for minimizing the impact of such problems. LSB also looks for management systems that maximize information flow from the contractor to LSB, ability to maintain budget control, and flexibility in dealing with political issues. LSB typically seeks the advice of the contractor's previous clients to judge the contractor's handling of budget and timing problems, track record on responsiveness, and quality of final products. LSB may also review *curriculum vitae* and consult with organizations that have worked with the contractor before.

Each new follow-up survey is also contracted for on a competitive basis, which gives LSB the opportunity to assess the contractor's performance and terminate the relationship if performance has been substandard.

The Client's Role in Conducting the Survey

LSB does not engage in data-collection activities but does exercise a high degree of control over how NORC collects and processes data. Since the relationship is contractual, LSB can specify, both in the RFP and in the contract, certain goals for response rates and quality control. NORC is expected to adhere to these standards. For example, the Center for Education Statistics has a policy requiring all surveys to achieve an 85 percent response rate. High School and Beyond has always had response-rate targets of 92 percent and has achieved response rates of at least 90 percent or higher.

The data-collection phase is the part of the survey in which the contractor operates with the greatest autonomy. NORC recruits, trains, and deploys hundreds of interviewers. Decisions are made about when interviewers should abandon attempts to collect responses to questionnaires and initiate the more costly telephone and personal interviews. NORC is expected to have the expertise and management systems that permit central office staff, field managers, and interviewers to exercise discretion in choosing which respondents to pursue, while still attempting to reach high response-rate levels in all sample cells.

Regarding quality control, each HS&B contract stipulates that the contractor submit for approval plans for receipt-control procedures, editing and coding of questionnaires, and data-cleaning routines. For example, in the most recent survey (the third follow-up), a computer-assisted data-entry system was used for coding open-ended items and keying numeric items. Ranges were established and loaded into the system so that outliers resulting from respondent and/or coder errors would be prevented. LSB approved all ranges before the system was used.

At the end of the survey, LSB works closely with NORC to ensure that public-use data tapes are as "user friendly" as possible. Data layout, composite variables, and the contents of the user's manuals are all specified. LSB staff are frequent analysts of the data, and LSB often provides useful composite variables for the contractor to append to the final data files. All files are delivered in raw form, with appropriate code for creating analysis files.

LSB carries out quality-control checks on all delivered tapes. This process involves having several staff members conduct analyses, using a portion of a tape's variables that relates to the policy interest at hand. This final review by knowledgeable users allows last-minute improvements that enhance the "user friendliness" of the publicly released data tapes.

Analysis and Reporting

During the base year of HS&B, NORC had a contractually specified responsibility for producing substantive analyses. Within the first year after data were collected, Coleman, Hoffer, and Kilgore (1981) completed their now famous report on public and private schools. DiPrete and Muller (1981) investigated discipline and order in American high schools, Lewin-Epstein (1981) reported on youth employment during high school, and Nielsen and Fernandez (1981) analyzed the achievement of Hispanic students.

Since that time, NORC's role in analysis has been limited to producing tabulations and capsule descriptions. The latter furnish highlights from each survey and indicate principal activities of the 1980 seniors and sophomores, changes in family status, military service, and shifts in life goals.

LSB staff currently assume the major role for analysis of results. They conduct in-house analyses and monitor analysis contracts. Most in-house analyses produce tabulations of data in anticipation of policy questions. Like many government agencies, LSB analysts also respond to urgent requests from policymakers. These requests frequently require extracting the needed data, producing a crosstab or table, and graphically displaying the findings in as short a time as one day.

LSB monitors three types of analysis contracts: comprehensive, shared staff, and task order/tabulation. Comprehensive analysis contracts generally are large, and the contractor provides all staff and data-processing expertise. Two major comprehensive analyses were recently completed with HS&B data: a study of high school offerings and enrollments, and a study of cognitive growth during high school. Shared-staff contracts involve both the analysis contractor and LSB staff; that is, the contractor assigns a single staff person, who is an expert in the analysis topic, to work with an LSB staff person, who completes all the computing tasks. About twelve shared-staff contracts have been completed with HS&B data. Finally, LSB has a task order/tabulation contractor who completes narrowly focused analyses, producing tabulations and reports of about twenty to thirty pages. Topics for analysis are selected by a consensus process similar to that used for developing specifications for data collection.

LSB and NORC have different viewpoints on whether it is appropriate for a data-collection contractor to carry out substantive analyses. LSB currently has a policy of separating data-collection contracts from analysis contracts, partly because of the belief that many survey organizations may not have staff skilled in undertaking analyses of results. Also, survey organizations, according to this view, are not equipped to deal with the fast pace of responding to questions from such policymakers as the secretary of education or Congress in the time frame allowed; without frequent close contact, survey organizations are not felt to have the knowledge of policy needs that would be required. In addition, during the base year, the analysis tasks required more effort and expense than had originally been anticipated, and there was intense controversy surrounding release of the public and private schools report. It is clear that part of LSB's reluctance to award analysis contracts to data-collection contractors results from the base-year experience. LSB's concern is that if analysis and data collection were to be combined in one contract, then any problems with the analysis could spread to other parts of the contract. Since final data-processing and analysis activities can occur simultaneously, disagreements over analysis could result in delays in the delivery of the data.

In contrast, NORC maintains that it has considerable capability and experience in conducting substantive research. There are several programmatic research centers within the organization, each staffed by recognized scholars in education, sociology, economics, political science, and other disciplines. With respect to the potential spread of analysis problems to other contract activities, a management structure could be established to keep activities separate and restrict any interference between tasks. Regarding urgent requests from policymakers for data, NORC agrees that LSB is better suited for responding quickly.

No attempt is made here to resolve these differences. Both LSB and NORC recognize that there are advantages and disadvantages to coupling data-collection contracts and analysis contracts. Separating them might promote more diversity in interpretation, since a fresh point of view would be brought in by the second contractor, but this might also produce greater start-up costs because new users must become familiar with large, complex data sets. Combining data collection and analysis could lead to more timely reporting of the data because within a single organization it is easier to merge the two activities. During the base year, for example, results were available in record time: less than a year after the end of data collection.

Aside from the decoupling issue, there is an additional consideration in awarding analysis projects, which has to do with the funding mechanism. LSB currently funds all outside work through contracts that are less conducive than grants are to fostering the kinds of independence needed to produce significant analyses. Grants would be a more appropriate vehicle, but LSB does not have the authority for funneling grant funds to researchers. Everyone would like to see HS&B used again for landmark analyses like those completed by Coleman, Hoffer, and Kilgore (1981), but it is not clear how best to encourage such work.

Promoting Use of the Data

NORC's responsibility for promoting use of the data is to generate data tapes that are well documented and readily used. At a minimum, there should be no technical barriers to their use. Beyond this, LSB is the primary actor in promoting use of the data. LSB delivers data to offices inside and out of the department that were supporters or interested parties from the time of the early position papers and RFPs. Data are supplied without charge to the Department of Education line offices and to the government offices and departments already mentioned. In addition, an announcement of the availability of the tapes goes out to over 1,200 persons. After each survey wave, tapes and user's manuals are sold at nominal cost to researchers across the country. These tapes are then copied and shared among colleagues. Generally, from 250 to 300 researchers purchase the tapes. After the first follow-up, 700 user's manuals were sold; thus, a good deal of tape sharing occurred among users.

The capsule descriptions are also designed to generate interest in the surveys and encourage researchers to obtain and utilize the data. The Center for Education Statistics printed and distributed 10,000 of the base-year HS&B capsule descriptions and 7,000 of the first follow-up capsule descriptions. The second follow-up capsule descriptions are currently being distributed. The Center for Education Statistics generally provides over 250 complimentary copies to Department of Education officials, Congress, state officials, and other federal agencies.

To enhance interest in the data, LSB staff have presented papers at major conventions and meetings. Specifically, they have spoken at meetings of the American Education Research Association, the American Sociology Association, the American Statistical Association, the American Council on Education, the National Institute of Independent Colleges and Universities, the American Association of Community and Junior Colleges, and the National Association of Student Financial Aid Administrators.

Finally, LSB staff have developed several analysis files, or special data tapes, that are designed to further enhance the "user friendliness" of the HS&B data. Analysis files are available for cognitive test data, parental financial data, postsecondary access and persistence data, student financial aid data, and the classification data used by LSB staff for tabulations.

Summary and Conclusions

In contracting for High School and Beyond, LSB seeks a partner in designing and carrying out each survey. Although in the base year NORC assisted LSB in defining policy issues and undertaking analyses of the data, in recent years LSB has assumed more of those responsibilities, especially that of analysis. Table 1 summarizes the major survey tasks and the various actors involved at each stage.

The arrangement under which the HS&B surveys are developed and conducted may not fit traditional views of client and evaluator roles. LSB is not operating a program or formulating educational policy, nor is NORC assisting with an evaluation study or a policy analysis. Instead, LSB and NORC together play the role of evaluator/policy researcher in creating a longitudinal data base and performing analyses related to educational policy. Recently, Wargo (in Hendricks, 1986, p. 24) ventured a definition of evaluation that indicates the growing similarity of evaluation and policy analysis and also sounds very much like what happens at HS&B: "a process of gathering, synthesizing, and analyzing information for persons who make decisions regarding policy or program operations."

At different phases of the survey, LSB and NORC each have relatively more or less responsibility. Both have participated in the identification of policy issues to be addressed by HS&B, with LSB having the major role in this area. Both have also shared in survey design. Once the contract is awarded, NORC takes the lead in sample design, instrument development, field testing, approval from the Office of Management and Budget, data collection and preparation, and construction and documen-

Table 1. Tasks by Actors

Task	LSB	LSB's Clients	NORC
Identify policy issues	Ascertains policy concerns of Dept. of Education and others	Formulate policy questions; react to position papers and RFPs	Assists LSB in identification of policy concerns
Generate survey design	Establishes parameters of design; works with NORC on final design	React to position papers and RFPs	Details methods and procedures in proposal and refines them further during contract period
Select contractor	Coordinates competitive bidding and evaluation of proposals	Send representatives to proposal-review panels	
Conduct field test and main survey	Sets standards; reviews instruments and procedures; monitors, performs quality control		Draws sample; develops instruments; conducts field test; collects data for main study; constructs and documents data files
Analysis	Conducts and commissions analyses; disseminates results		At times carries out analyses
Interpretation/policy studies	Responds to data requests	Incorporate data in policy studies of programmatic areas	

tation of the data files. Nevertheless, LSB maintains considerable control over these activities, continually reviewing NORC's performance, refining specifications, and monitoring expenditures.

LSB currently assumes the most active role in analysis. LSB staff and their analysis contractors generate tabulations and reports and distribute them to groups who express interest in these topics in the first place. In addition, LSB responds regularly to new questions and data requests from policymakers.

Although their partnership implies harmony and cooperation between LSB and NORC, at time the relationship is subject to tension, which arises as the two organizations try to accommodate their own separate interests. NORC attempts to keep the scope of work within the budget and schedule limitations imposed by the contract. LSB is concerned that survey design and content remain flexible and therefore responsive to changing interests in policy research. The balance between cooperation and tension is healthy in that it prevents excessive cooperation, which could lead to co-optation. At the same time, there is sufficient sharing of goals to restrain conflict, which could ultimately lead to low productivity.

One of the strengths of the current arrangement is that it capitalizes on the capabilities of each partner. LSB is strategically situated for keeping abreast of the most salient policy debates, the schedules for reauthorization of programs, the policy initiatives that may be under way, and the routine information needs of the department. These understandings inform the survey design. NORC, with its technical and managerial staff, national field staff, and data-processing department, has the capability for designing and conducting the survey. Once the data are final, LSB can again make use of its insights into current policy debate to generate reports, tabulations, and special studies that meet the information needs of the department.

The division of labor between LSB and NORC is ultimately pragmatic in that it produces an organizational structure that facilitates policy research. Nevertheless, the current role structure tends to ignore broader uses of the data. There is little to encourage scrutiny of the data by leading scholars and substantive specialists in education and other disciplinary fields. Certainly, the tapes are available at relatively low cost to researchers, and after each survey wave, hundreds take advantage of them. There might be greater payback, however, in terms of use of the data if there were more broad-based funding of significant investigations designed to contribute to the knowledge base in secondary education, postsecondary and higher education, and the needs of the nation's youth. Currently, both budgetary and regulatory obstacles inhibit such activity.

52

References

Coleman, J. S., Bartot, V., Lewin-Epstein, N., and Olson, L. *Policy Issues and Research Design*. Chicago: National Opinion Research Center, University of Chicago, 1979.

Coleman, J. S., Hoffer, T., and Kilgore, S. *Public and Private Schools: An Analysis of High School and Beyond*. Washington, D.C.: National Center for Education Statistics, 1981.

DiPrete, T. A., and Muller, C. *Discipline and Order in American High Schools*. Washington, D.C.: National Center for Education Statistics, 1981.

Hendricks, M. "A Conversation with Michael Wargo." *Evaluation Practice*, 1986, 7 (4), 23–34.

Lewin-Epstein, N. *Youth Employment During High School: An Analysis of High School and Beyond*. Washington, D.C.: National Center for Education Statistics, 1981.

Nielsen, F., and Fernandez, R. M. *Achievement of Hispanic Students in American High Schools: Background Characteristics and Achievement*. Washington, D.C.: National Center for Education Statistics, 1981.

Penny A. Sebring is a survey director at NORC, University of Chicago.

C. Dennis Carroll is chief of Longitudinal Studies Branch, Center for Education Statistics, U.S. Department of Education.

*A strategy is proposed and described for sharing evaluation
responsibilities between client and evaluator, thereby leveraging
the evaluator consultant's time and expertise and
minimizing cost.*

Large-Scale Evaluation
on a Limited Budget:
The Partnership Experience

Jonathan Z. Shapiro, David L. Blackwell

This chapter describes the design and implementation of a partnership
evaluation at Southeastern Louisiana University in Hammond, Louisiana, during the 1985–86 academic year. The first author of this paper
was introduced to the term (and notion of) *partnership evaluation* while
working for the Office of Evaluation Research in the College of Education, University of Illinois at Chicago. The director of the office, Harriet
Talmage, used the term to describe an arrangement between evaluators
and clients in which many roles traditionally undertaken by external
evaluators—such as formulation of specific evaluation questions, instrument design, and data collection—were either shared or fully taken on by
evaluation clients. The major focus of this chapter is on the nature and
consequences, both intended and unintended, of just such a partnership
relationship. The first author of this chapter (Shapiro) functioned as the
external evaluator on the project. The second author (Blackwell), who
directed the project, became the internal advocate of evaluation. The
project, a Title III "Strengthening Institutions" program, involved six
activity areas. Thus the major actors in the evaluation were the external
evaluator, the internal advocate, and the activity directors. This chapter

J. Nowakowski (ed.). *The Client Perspective on Evaluation.*
New Directions for Program Evaluation, no. 36. San Francisco: Jossey-Bass, Winter 1987.

attempts to describe the external and internal perspectives on the sequence of events, as well as the meaning of the partnerships that emerged during the evaluation.

Origins of the Evaluation

Southeastern Louisiana University (SLU) was awarded its four-year Title III grant in 1982. The overall objective of the grant was to strengthen major components of the university so as to make it a sound institution in the mainstream of higher education. To accomplish this objective, SLU identified six areas that required special attention: an electronic learning laboratory, a development foundation, comprehensive counseling center, business education, industrial technology instruction, and chemistry–physics instruction.

Blackwell: Two years into the project, the granting agency began to talk about objective, quantifiable outcomes data. At the same time, I was sensing the need for continued agency funding and university support. The need and the desire for evaluation on my part were intense, but resources were limited. At this time, one of the project's activity directors put me in contact with Dr. Shapiro. We met to discuss the feasibility of conducting an evaluation under these budgetary conditions, with the additional constraint that none of the activity directors was familiar with program evaluation; they certainly did not share my perceived need for such activities.

Shapiro: When I met with Dr. Blackwell, he described the situation at SLU as one of unlimited information needs, limited resources, and almost no available resident technical expertise in evaluation. He asked if anything could be done under those circumstances, and I raised the possibility of a partnership approach, with the program personnel taking on many of the evaluation activities and responsibilities themselves. I suggested this cooperative strategy because the funds for a complete external evaluation were lacking, the evaluation needed to cover six different knowledge bases, and the dynamics of client control and investment might improve the attitudes of the activity directors toward program evaluation.

The Proposed Evaluation Strategy

S: After meeting with Dr. Blackwell, I agreed to submit a plan for partnership evaluation. Because there was little resident knowledge about program evaluation, I proposed to conduct a half-day workshop with the activity directors on program evaluation, assign each director to decide what type of evaluation information he or she wished to generate, and then meet with each director for two hours to assist in the development of individual research plans.

B: After speaking with Dr. Shapiro and receiving his evaluation proposal, I had to sell the idea of partnership evaluation to the activity directors. I emphasized that evaluation was necessary, financial resources were limited, and partnership evaluation was a possibility. I admitted the techniques and implications of partnership evaluation were not totally clear to me: We would be exploring new territory together, making up some of the rules as we went along. The staff agreed unanimously to have the evaluator visit the university and give a presentation on partnership evaluation.

Implementation of the Partnership Process

S: When agreement had been reached on the initial evaluation activities, I came to SLU to present an evaluation workshop to the activity directors. The workshop included a brief history of program evaluation; a discussion of what program evaluation can and cannot do; an introduction to instrument construction, data collection, and data analysis; and a description of what the activity directors would be responsible for in the partnership before meeting with the external evaluator.

B: After the presentation, I assured the activity directors that they were not obligated to participate, but that limited funds were available to those who wanted to work with the external evaluator. Each activity director was encouraged to arrange a two-hour meeting with the external evaluator, to discuss his or her responsibilities and the responsibilities of the evaluator.

S: The heart of the partnership infrastructure was developed during the series of individual planning meetings. Every activity director, as well as the project director, met with me; however, the director in business education decided to evaluate his activity independently. The approach to evaluation design on my part required flexibility and reaction, rather than proaction, because the activity director initially was to determine the course and goals of the evaluation research project. Because the projects were individualized, there was significant variation from project to project in terms of the amount of inquiry activity; the relative effort required of the external evaluator, the activity director, and the activity staff; and the complexity of the evaluation research techniques and data that were generated.

In discussions with the Activity Directors, some ground rules were established that were constant across designs. The directors had to specify the purpose of the evaluation research (tempered by the external evaluator's input concerning the limits of social science research methodology). The directors were responsible for identifying the important affective and cognitive dimensions to be measured in the respective program areas. All instruments developed by the external evaluator were treated as draft forms. The directors had the final authority to determine questions, coding procedures, length, and other characteristics. The directors were responsible for overseeing the collection of data, although the evaluator had the sole responsibility for analyzing the data. Finally, individual evaluation was to be presented in draft form to the director, who could edit it and, if necessary, negotiate its final form with the external evaluator.

B: During this series of meetings, my role as the internal advocate for evaluation became very important. It was here that the partnership would be developed or abandoned. At this point, there were people on the staff who felt that the evaluator was being employed to "do it all." I had to explain very carefully that the partnership evaluation called for a lot of evaluation, with reduced expenditures and magnified staff involvement. I announced my desire to participate in the evaluation along with the activity directors by evaluating the overall administration of the grant. This statement helped to decrease the time it took for trust to develop within the partnership. It also signalled that, as project director, I was willing to work, and that I felt challenged to enter a new dimension of evaluation responsibility. Since I met weekly with each activity director, I was able to serve as a liaison to the external evaluator, the activity directors, and the university administrators.

S: The six individual evaluation research plans, written by five of the activity directors and the project director, were quite varied in purpose, scope, activity, and relative effort (see Table 1). The evaluation of the grant administration focused on two questions. At the beginning of the academic year, a needs assessment of the activity directors was conducted. It concerned how the project director should function to assist them. At the end of the year, an attitude survey was administered to various people in the university. It concerned the performance of the project director during the year. The evaluation of the electronic learning laboratory was based on two quasi-experiments, one of which assessed the impact of computer-assisted instruction on writing and one of which assessed its impact on mathematics.

The evaluation of the comprehensive counseling center focused on demographic characteristics of clients, which were correlated with an intake assessment instrument administered on a pre- and posttreatment basis. The evaluation of the development foundation consisted of a pretest and a posttest attitude survey that was mailed to a stratified random sample of faculty and staff. Its purpose was to determine the degree to which awareness of the foundation's activities and attitudes toward the foundation had changed during the year.

The evaluation of chemistry–physics instruction involved assessing the impact of newly purchased scientific equipment on students' ability to conduct and understand chemistry experiments. Finally, the evaluation of industrial technology instruction was based on a survey of recent graduates with respect to their assessment of the program's ability to provide them with the competencies required for success in their various professional fields.

B: As the partnership developed, trust was built, so that all partners began to feel that they could open up and share, without fear of being hurt. No longer was there an idea that the external evaluator would "do it all." It was important for the external *partner* (no longer "the evaluator") to know that the atmosphere at the university was changing. New vice-presidents had been hired, merit pay was a topic of major concern, and promotion and tenure policies were being rewritten. All these issues affected the staff's motivation for participating in an evaluation. These issues could be discussed within the partnership, but an external evaluator under contract might never have learned or been interested in learning about them.

Partners were encouraged to call the external partner and to ask questions and supply information about their projects. They were assured that their input was important and that it would be reflected in the methodology. For example, before any instruments for data collection were developed, much time was spent discussing the desired outcomes, the most cost-effective way of obtaining the data, and the need to eliminate items that appeared politically inappropriate because of timing or other organizational issues.

What Was Learned About Partnership Evaluation

S: In reflecting on the year-long experience at SLU, we have been impressed by several salient aspects of the nature, benefits, and costs of the partnership approach. From the procedural perspective, it is clear that accepting the role of external partner in an evaluation project requires the evaluator to operate in a less conventional and more collaborative manner. The external evaluator must work consciously to lessen the sense of ownership that often accompanies an evaluation project. One cannot impose a research design, a statistical technique, a locally constructed instrument, or even a "good idea" when the prespecified ground rules give substantial responsibility and authority to the client.

Even more than usual, the evaluator must develop sensitivity to the advice and criticism of partners—a crucial element of partnership evaluation if the client is truly going to act and feel like a partner. I must admit that at times the constant criticism to which my instrument drafts (approximately fifteen local constructions) were subjected became tiresome, particularly because the more the partners criticized, the better they got at it. I had to keep in mind, however, that such criticism would not only improve the evaluation but also bond the partners to the evalu-

Table 1. A Summary of Activities in the SLU Partnership Evaluation

Activity Area	Evaluation Project	External Partner's Role	Internal Partner's Role
Grant administration	Needs assessment	Design draft of needs-assessment questionnaire	Make final decision on form of questionnaire
		Content-analyze questionnaire data	Identify sample; mail out questionnaire
	Assessment of performance	Design draft of attitude survey	Make final decision on form of survey
		Collect and analyze survey data	Identify sample; mail out survey
Electronic learning laboratory	Impact of computer-assisted instruction on writing	Design writing-assessment protocol	Identify treatments
		Collect and analyze protocol data	Assign instructors and classes to treatment
			Obtain student essays from instructors
	Impact of computer-assisted instruction on mathematics	Analyze mathematics achievement data	Identify treatment
			Assign instructors and classes to treatment
			Obtain student achievement data and ACT scores
Comprehensive counseling center	Gains on psychological intake instrument	Develop draft of client demographic and attitude survey	Make final decision on survey form
		Analyze survey and intake data	Develop intake instrument
			Administer intake pre- and posttests

Table 1. *(continued)*

Activity Area	Evaluation Project	External Partner's Role	Internal Partner's Role
			Collect survey data
			Obtain retention and GPA data from office of institutional research
Development foundation	Pretest/posttest survey on changes in knowledge of and attitudes toward the foundation	Develop draft of survey	Make final decision on form of survey
		Analyze pretest/posttest data	With office of institutional research, identify a stratified random sample
			Mail out pretest/posttest survey forms
Chemistry–physics instruction	Impact of new equipment on conduct of laboratory experiments	Develop draft of observation form and student attitude survey	Make final decision on form of observation instrument and attitude survey
		Analyze observation, attitude, and achievement data	Devise and implement observation schedule
			Collect data on student attitudes, achievement, GPA, and ACT scores
Industrial technology	Survey of graduates	Collection of survey data	Total development of questionnaire
		Analysis of survey data	Identification of sample
			Data collection

ation process: They, too, "owned" the instruments. In fact, knowing that the instrumentation would be subject to partnership review made the development easier to undertake. Whenever I could not come to satisfactory decisions—for example, on the best coding scheme to use for a particular instrument—I knew that the partners would be obligated to assist in making final choices.

A second difference of partnership is that the external evaluator must take on the role of "evaluation educator" at a much more self-conscious level than usual. This is true not only with respect to formal instruction (for example, the introductory workshop) but also with respect to the constant barrage of questions, comments, insights, and reflections that clients may offer while planning and carrying out individual evaluation projects. Ignorance is not bliss when the client undertakes his or her partnership obligation seriously; thus, I found myself spending much more time explaining, justifying, and even defending evaluation theory, practice, and philosophy than I would have done in a conventional evaluation. At times, the external evaluator takes on a sort of mentorship role in working with clients on their own evaluations. In this regard, the single most painful experience I had was in teaching a day-long workshop on classroom observation to a group of chemists and physicists (skeptics all) prior to their conducting observations on the frustration levels exhibited by students using old versus new laboratory equipment. I spent most of the morning explaining to these bench scientists how observed student behavior could be considered data. Those who were interested in learning about ethnographic methods returned after lunch. Ultimately, nineteen faculty observations of several chemistry experiments became a major and strong component of the evaluation of chemistry–physics instruction.

Interestingly, one unintended consequence of implementing a partnership evaluation was learning a great deal about the hidden agenda, the unquestioned assumptions, and the accepted roles and relationships adopted by evaluators and clients in more traditional evaluation arrangements. For example, subjecting myself to partnership-based criticism of instruments made me realize that when I am involved in a conventional evaluation and the construction of local instruments is required, I never consider asking clients to pass judgment on the instruments, and they almost never do so on their own. Similarly, the traditional political power arrangement between evaluator and client leads to expectations that the choice of research design, statistical techniques, and data interpretation are the province of the evaluation expert; neither evaluator nor client expects much questioning of the evaluator's decisions. In effect, the conscious decision to engage in partnership evaluation means that the conventional power relationships will be altered, and this departure may have an unsettling effect on evaluator and client alike.

While the original impetus for conducting a partnership evaluation was economic, I am now convinced that no other approach would have been successful in the particular organizational and political context of this evaluation. This was a project that could not have been carried out unless an external evaluator had provided technical assistance and an internal advocate had been not only sensitive to university politics but also able to hold the project together until the external partner's relationships with individual activity directors had been solidified. Thus, the success of the project was due to the internal advocate's original and prior commitment to evaluation and to his willingness to support my activities, even when he was not quite sure what I was doing or attempting to do, until the individual activity directors were willing to trust me.

I assumed that the partnerships were going to be a series of dyads, but the reality turned out to be much more complicated. The partnerships had to be brokered by the internal advocate, and so first there was a central partnership between myself and him, concurrent with his initial partnership with the activity directors. Eventually I developed partnerships with the activity directors. Almost all of this process had escaped me until I heard the internal advocate present his perspective on the evaluation to a conference audience. He made me realize how unaware of subtle organizational dynamics an evaluator can be.

B: The role of the internal advocate was extremely important in the Title III evaluation. I was not surprised when the Title III staff did not respond positively to the original notion of evaluation, for it was a strange and unknown thing to most of them. Ironically, the staff tried to protect me from the evaluation process. When the survey of my performance as grant administrator went out to a sample of faculty and staff, with a cover letter bearing only the external evaluator's signature, several people came to assure me not to worry; they were not going to send the survey in and would not provide information regarding a colleague to an outsider. I had to inform them that the survey was my idea and that I wanted them to respond. I realized that the problem could have been avoided if the cover letter had carried my name on it as well as Dr. Shapiro's. This would have demonstrated that our partnership was important and provided compelling evidence that we really wanted sound information.

A partnership evaluation produces beneficial data when everyone is a true partner who wants to be involved for the purpose of obtaining useful information. Each partner must be willing to take a risk, patient about what he or she will get for the time and effort invested, and willing to provide information as input data.

The internal advocate must be in a position to understand the networking among those involved in the evaluation. He or she must maintain frequent contact and open communication with all staff and must hone negotiating skills so as to cultivate the development of a true partnership. Throughout the evaluation, the internal advocate must serve as a liaison, both to the staff and to the external partner, never forgetting to assure the staff that their input is needed and that no one is going to "do it to them." The internal advocate must also keep the external evaluator informed of other forces and events that may directly or indirectly influence the success of the evaluation. In summary, all partners must be willing to develop honest, open relationships to accomplish a common goal—a meaningful evaluation.

Jonathan Z. Shapiro is an associate professor of education at Louisiana State University. His research interests include program evaluation and policy analysis.

David L. Blackwell is director of sponsored research and contracts at Southeastern Louisiana University. His research interests include program evaluation and gerontological research. .

Taking clients' expectations into account enhances the
potential utility of the evaluator's efforts.

Lessons About
Clients' Expectations

Larry A. Braskamp, Dale C. Brandenburg,
John C. Ory

The purpose of this chapter is to summarize salient recurrent themes that
we have encountered in working with a variety of clients. Our generalizations are based on our experiences as staff in the Office of Instructional
and Management Services (IMS) at the University of Illinois at Urbana-
Champaign (UIUC) and as for-hire consultants to industry and other
institutions of higher learning.

Two divisions of IMS deal with providing information to clients.
The first office, Measurement and Evaluation (M&E), provides several
campus services, including instructor and course evaluation, computer
scoring and analysis of exams, placement and proficiency assessment,
and evaluations of campus or externally funded programs. As staff of
M&E, we have also conducted a number of ad hoc evaluation studies
targeted on such concerns as faculty turnover, support services for students with academic difficulties, the honors programs, and various service
agencies within the university. In addition, we provide information to
the periodic departmental review process that has been in operation for
the last twelve years on our campus.

The second office, Management Information, provides statistical

J. Nowakowski (ed.). *The Client Perspective on Evaluation.*
New Directions for Program Evaluation, no. 36. San Francisco: Jossey-Bass, Winter 1987.

and quantitative information to department heads, deans, vice chancellors, and the chancellor at the University of Illinois for their use. As coordinator of administrator evaluation, we have also provided consultative help to faculty committees that have evaluated over one hundred department heads, deans, and vice-chancellors on the UIUC campus. (In this chapter, the pronoun *we* will be used in discussing the work and experiences of one or more of the authors.)

As evaluation consultants, we have provided services to a number of consulting organizations (for example, LifeLong Learning and Metritech), educational institutions (for example, Indiana University and Wilkes College), and corporations (for example, Motorola, Boeing Commerical Airplane Company, and Coopers & Lybrand).

Our methods of collecting the data for this chapter varied. We used quotes and comments that we received informally from our clients, distributed formal surveys asking clients what they like and what they prefer to be included in an evaluation, and took excerpts from letters addressed to us and from public documents describing the intent of evaluations. We also conducted in-depth interviews with some clients, as well as several informal telephone surveys to provide information for this chapter.

What Clients Appear to Want from Evaluators

Some themes emerge from the diverse client responses we have encountered in over a decade of conducting evaluations. The themes presented in this chapter are not conclusions about clients' expectations, since not all clients agree. Moreover, the interpretations we give are what we as evaluators have heard and read and view as most important. They are important to us because we have been required to take them into account in order to be credible.

Objectivity

When working for clients as internal evaluators, we have been told of the need to be perceived as objective. Objectivity is important to the user because there has to be an appearance of credibility to the multiple audiences who receive or are affected by the evaluation. If an internal client such as a dean cannot be assured of this objectivity, then there will be little trust in the results. The evaluation itself also must often be presented to internal clients in an objective and unbiased fashion, so that they feel free to act or not act on the results. Internal clients do not want to be put in the position of having either to publicly accept or reject the proposed action. Some administrators do not regard evaluators as members of the "inner circle."

Evaluators are not decision makers, nor do they have access to all inside information. In fact, we recently were told candidly that entering into policy analysis and going beyond the current evaluation of a program would place us at risk of being "eaten alive" by some administrators. Our experience is that decision makers often feel they have to keep some distance from internal evaluators; a close personal relationship can be too compromising for the administrator. One college president stated, "I have to make sure that I have the ability to reject what persons do and say without having to worry that it is going to influence our personal relationship." From our perspective, here also lies a paradox: To promote effective use of an internal evaluation, the internal evaluators must gain the ear and the confidence of the "inner circle," knowing full well that they cannot become equal partners. The internal evaluator thus must rely on professional competence, objectivity, and clarity of presentation, rather than on personal relationships.

As evaluators, we present our ideas to planning teams and administrators. Usually we are not the decision makers. Some distance is maintained—not always by evaluators, but by those who use us; they want and accept the final responsibility for making decisions. It is both a privilege they wish to keep and a burden they choose not to place upon us. Simply put, we as internal evaluators are staff.

As external evaluators, we often have been hired to "guarantee" objectivity in the evaluation process. One client at a large manufacturing company consistently hires external evaluators because, as the managers explain, the evaluators are unbiased, and their "outside" information is more credible and more reliable. This client believes that external evaluators can take more heat and be less "buffaloed" than internal evaluators, and that external evaluators can "scare the hell out of people."

An external person can also collect information that otherwise might be difficult to obtain. In the words of one major university client, "the outsider can provide objective reflections on both sides of the issues, and the site visit gave an opportunity for some key individuals to vent their opinions." The result was considered both balanced and energizing. Thus, as external evaluators, we offer a sense of objectivity. We obtain and communicate information about sensitive topics that cannot be gained through the normal internal channels.

Evaluator Expertise and Practical Experience

Evaluator expertise and prior experience was an issue for all of our clients. In fact, such client expectations often became conditions for employment. One of our corporate clients explained his view: We had to have practical experience working with companies like his, and if he had to choose between two evaluators with similar academic expertise and credentials, he would always choose the one with more practical experience. Another client also preferred to work with evaluators who demonstrated content expertise and practical experience. He also told us that in one situation the evaluator's having published a book was considered important. We worked for one large corporation because, in the words of the client, "We realized that no one here had any expertise in that area, and we thought of you guys."

In sum, most of our clients select evaluators on the basis of experience and expertise. Clients prefer to work with evaluators who have previous experience with similar problems and in similar settings.

Understanding the Evaluation Context

Comprehension of the environmental setting in which evaluation is to take place is a common expectation of clients. Evaluators need to acknowledge the organizational environment and take it into account in their evaluation activities. For example, one of our clients was a manufacturing company involved in different businesses. We were expected to acquire knowledge of the products and operations at each type of business if we were to understand how training could function and subsequently how evaluation of training might be reported. The client wanted us to understand how people at each factory site perceived the corporate training office and the credibility of each field training site. "It is critical," said our client "to be very sensitive to the environment, because the environment dictates the message of both what is said and how it is said."

From other colleges and universities, we often receive requests that appear initially to be simple. These clients often say, "We want you to evaluate the revision to our evaluation process and tell us what you think about it." In our discussions with them, it becomes apparent that they want to make certain we understand the context in which the evaluation process is developed. For example, those at small colleges want some indication of our sensitivity to local needs and situations—for example, a small number of faculty in a department who know each other very well.

Implications for Action

This issue involves expected roles and functions of the evaluator. Does the evaluator describe, analyze, interpret, recommend, and present one or several possible intervention strategies or solutions to an identified problem? From our experiences, we believe evaluators should include a set of recommendations, whether working internally or externally. For example, one vice-chancellor requested a single set of recommendations logically derived from the evaluation, so that there would be a plan of action to which he could react. Another administrator wanted to see several proposed alternative solutions, believing that if we evaluators were going to spend considerable time studying the program, then we should have some ideas about how to remedy problems. A client at a large manufacturing company told us that evaluators must be responsible for making recommendations. He stated, "I don't believe data ever speak for themselves. Only evaluators know what the results are. I need recommendations. I expect them. You're only half done if no recommendations are made." Another of our corporate clients merely said that recommendations must be included.

Once included, recommendations must be viewed by clients as practical for enhancing the utility of the evaluation report. In an evaluation of a campus service organization, we carefully examined its impact on campus and recommended two alternatives to its current operation. The main user, a vice-chancellor, indicated that while the report was insightful and increased his understanding of the program, he had difficulty knowing what to do next. As far as he was concerned, neither of the two options presented was practical, and both evaluator and administrator were frustrated over the utility of the report.

We have learned that often the first question to be asked in designing evaluations for clients is "So what? If we collect this information, what behaviors can be changed, what actions can be taken, and what decisions will be affected by it?" This action-oriented emphasis is especially salient with corporate and consulting clients who want solutions in very practical terms. Increased understanding is generally not a sufficient reason; in a sense, this issue is of most importance because these clients have identified a problem for which they want some alternative recommended solutions, without which they will not make an investment. For example, in our work with a consulting company that advises health care organizations, we often heard the consultant/client state, "I cannot give a diagnosis to someone without providing a prescription. That just makes the client more worried."

To many clients, especially those in business, if there is no linkage between the evaluation and management decisions, the information collected has little or no perceived utility. That linkage often takes the form of recommendations about management practices and intervention strategies. It is important to know the extent of proposed actions to be prescribed by the evaluator.

Sensitivity to Clients' Needs

As a service unit on campus, we give students a rating form to evaluate the instructional competence of faculty. Multiple and conflicting uses of the information occur. Faculty use the information for improving courses and teaching styles, but administrators use it to make annual salary decisions, as well as promotion and tenure decisions. These conflicting purposes have resulted in many controversies on our campus and at other colleges about what kinds of information should be required and who should see it. Department chairpersons have told us that they prefer not to see a normative interpretation of student ratings, because young assistant professors who are just beginning to teach seldom receive high ratings initially. It is difficult to counsel a young faculty member who is devastated by being rated in the bottom decile. Many departmental administrators prefer instead to view the responses from an absolute rather than a relative perspective. Faculty, however, repeatedly tell us that the most useful information for them is not the scaled responses. They often become discouraged; a score of 5.1 on a 6-point scale still puts one below average, as compared with other professors. Professors most often use students' written comments because those are particularly relevant to teaching behavior.

As internal evaluators, we must attempt to satisfy different audiences who have different needs and purposes for our evaluative information. Sometimes we must also address changes in clients' needs over time.

For the last ten years, department heads, deans, and vice-chancellors at UIUC have received in-depth periodic evaluations in which input from faculty is required. Although the program is not uniformly conducted in all colleges, we provide suggestions to committees on how to conduct the evaluations. In 1983, we formally commented on the vice-chancellor's suggestion that the principal intent of these evaluations was for administrative purposes. "The primary purpose of these evaluations," we said, "is to deliver a useful and trustworthy evaluation to the administrator to whom the person being evaluated reports." We added that the second use was to give administrators information to help them understand their leadership competencies and promote "a more productive working relationship between the unit faculty and staff and the administrator being evaluated." Thus, through the vice-chancellor, we have switched from a primary, or almost sole, emphasis on summative evaluation to formative evaluation, which gives much more consideration to the person being evaluated. In 1986, the vice-chancellor said in a letter to one of the committees, "This review should be conducted with a spirit of cooperation and constructive criticism," adding that the most "productive and beneficial" evaluations involve both the dean's and the faculty's input and help the dean to enlarge or improve leadership.

Standardizing the Presentation of Data

In our development of evaluation programs and procedures on our campus, there has been and continues to be client tension over the extent to which the procedures are uniform and standardized. Many reasons for standardization have been offered by evaluators and central campus staff. One is ease and efficiency of operation; that is, the same method of data collection and the same report format make the process more efficient. Moreover, the users, especially those on faculty committees, can more easily understand reports if the same results are presented consistently in the same format. Because the campuswide review committee on all promotion and tenure cases had problems with interpreting the student ratings, the vice-chancellor for academic affairs issued a directive during the summer of 1986 to all faculty considered for promotion and tenure saying that henceforth they should use the results from the students' standardized rating system in documenting their own effectiveness as teachers. Although approximately 85 percent of the assistant professors were already employing this campuswide rating system, there has been considerable controversy regarding the practical and philosophical consequences of this new directive. For example, one college requested that this communication be suspended for a year to examine more seriously how evaluations of teaching quality fit into appropriate reviews for promotion and tenure. One of its deans argued that both the common form and the normative information would promote "the idea that average teaching is acceptable." (We should note that our evaluation office has never claimed that norm-based student ratings ought to be the sole source of evaluative information on teaching. We argue just the opposite and advocate a multipurpose criterion-source method of evaluation [Braskamp, Brandenburg, and Ory, 1984].)

The standardization theme has also emerged with the use of our campus profile by administrators on our campus. The campus profile gives information for the past ten years about each academic and administrative unit in the university. It includes quantitative information about budgets, expenditures, student majors, faculty, nonacademic staff, and credit hours produced. The Division of Management Information also provides these data in a Lotus 1-2-3 spreadsheet format, so that departments can individually manipulate them or easily make graphs and tables. These types of data have been described as the "golden data base" by campus-level administrators, who now have the same information on each unit, and arguments about which data bases to use have largely been eliminated. Each unit administrator should be more accountable, since indicators of productivity and efficiency are widely available, and everyone can now discuss inferences about quality and effectiveness. This reasoning is not always accepted on campus, however. A notable critique came to us in a letter from a senior faculty member regarding our first campus profile. An excerpt from his letter follows:

> The classical definition of a university is *a collection of
> individual colleges.* In a healthy university, different colleges

have different missions, different character. They are in some ways similar, and on some occasions must be considered comparatively. As a technical specialist, you are obligated to facilitate those comparisons. But you are also obligated, I think, to frustrate simplistic comparisons and overdependency on comparison. On this campus we have not shown due restraint in using instructional unit data. Now with these profiles we may go another step toward management by glance.

Let us encourage our administrators to know their colleges thoroughly. I hope that you will find ways of cautioning data users against overuse, of reminding them of the great amount of omitted information, and of preserving the idea that it is healthy to have distinctive as well as distinguished colleges.

As internal evaluators, we become caught between two factions: central administrators, who see the value of standardization for comparative interpretations; and clients from the various units, who see standardized evaluation information as insensitive to work performed and thus impeding rather than promoting excellence and quality.

Comprehensibility

Client understanding of an evaluation report is critical, especially for more influential clients within the organization. For example, a member of the board of trustees told us several years ago, "If we [the board] cannot understand what is in a report, it is due primarily to the inability of the writer to clearly present the ideas, rather than our lack of intelligence." More recently, a consultant working with a large hospital commented to the evaluator who had written a report intended for discussion by the chief executive officer and his staff, "I see you are using the words *independent* and *dependent variable* in the report. Please eliminate them immediately and never use those words. If so, we will not be able to work with [the clients] on a long-term basis." A dedicated research scientist has also poked fun at a report in which one of our colleagues made repeated references to the importance of an "educational experience." He jokingly wanted to know the difference between a regular experience and an educational one. To him, this was jargon, which reduced his opinion of the writer's ability to communicate clearly to those who are not members of a particular discipline.

In our campus debate over the use of students' evaluations of teaching for all promotion and tenure documentation, a vice-chancellor wrote a letter to faculty who wished to postpone the implementation of the requirement until further study on the evaluation of teaching. "Just this week," he said, "I reviewed the file of a nontenured faculty member from a unit that does not use [the evaluations]; it was impossible for me, or anyone on my staff, to be able to interpret the meaning of the scores offered from the student evaluations. Nor could we understand, on the basis of the data provided, whether the narrative claims made by the department about the faculty member's teaching correlated in any way with the student evaluations. It was frankly impossible, from the file, to determine whether the person was a good, average, or poor teacher. I suspect that the confusion generated by the file may have tried to mask some rather mediocre teaching."

The comprehensibility of data analysis and results is likewise important. One senior university official told us, "I prefer statistical results I can understand, rather than those that are derived. I do not trust scores that I do not understand. Besides, derived scores really have no reality base." Another told us, "I want to see the raw data as well as the summary statistics. Only then can I get an adequate understanding of the diversity of opinion."

Evaluation information may be rendered uninterpretable by lack of clarity and use of ambiguous terms. A report that is not easily understood by a client can be interpreted in a number of ways. There is inherently more risk in such a report for both the client and the evaluator.

Credible Sources

We have learned that an evaluation report needs to be not only objective but also credible to the various audiences. This is of most concern to those who request an evaluation. However, the definition of *credible information* is not uniformly agreed upon by all potential clients and audiences. From our experience, the credibility of information is often dependent on its source. As one example, our administrator evaluation process differs according to how the confidentiality of information is treated. Our suggestion to committees conducting administrator evaluations included this statement: "This purpose can best be served if a high degree of confidentiality about the contents of the evaluation is preserved. Thus, the distribution of the evaluation should be carefully considered. The vice-chancellor has endorsed the principle that only those with a need to know should have access to the report."

If faculty members responding to the evaluation do not provide their signatures, some administrators argue that those faculty are not acting professionally. College deans, in reviewing evaluations of departmental heads, have questioned the meaningfulness and accuracy of unsigned reviews. Assessments without attribution were discounted, especially if the opinion was unusually negative or vitriolic. Furthermore, it was argued, this "secret ballot" system gives equal weight to junior and senior faculty, which sometimes has led to considerable misunderstanding in the absence of background knowledge for certain administrative decisions.

Another example of the credibility of information deriving from its source comes from our experience with a corporate client. For one portion of our evaluation, we needed to collect realistic dollar estimates of the value of training. Some collected figures were treated at face value (no cross-checking), depending on who provided the amounts. In other cases, we had to document in very specific terms how dollar amounts were derived and verify the amounts through a second source. Thus, credibility of source is different from reliability. Client trust is built by collecting data from the "right" sources, regardless of method employed.

Conciseness

Conciseness and brevity are commonly expected and highly regarded by our clients, both inside and outside the university. One chancellor has often told us, "I want to see the report in one page. If it cannot be put on one page, then it is not worth commenting on." A chief executive officer of a *Fortune* 500 company told us, "I will not read a report that is fatter than one-eighth of an inch thick." Still another corporate client warned us, "Many evaluators get caught up in 'evaluation' and can't get the message across—make it simple."

Timeliness

We have seen many situations in which the client's imposed timelines required us to analyze and interpret large amounts of data very quickly for the information to be most useful. One evaluation project with a large manufacturing company had loose overall time constraints, with the exception of individual site visits. Once we had completed a given site visit, the client expected a report in a few days, so that individuals at each site could review the findings while our visit was fresh in their minds. Thus, our internal confirmation of data prior to their general release required very tight timelines. As the client once remarked to us in reference to report transmission, "Regular U.S. mail just won't do." Another corporate client requested our assistance, provided we could develop a survey instrument "overnight." The client was meeting the next day with his government funding agent and anticipated the agent's eagerness to provide an instrument if one did not exist. Without an instrument in hand, the client would have had difficulty negotiating the types of data to be collected.

Clients need evaluative information when they have to make decisions, not afterward. Information submitted after a decision point is of little value. Therefore, evaluators must adhere to the timelines imposed by the client if they want their efforts to be of maximum value and utility.

Summary

What do clients expect of evaluators and their evaluation activities? What do clients expect of evaluation reports? Clients want an evaluator who has had experience with similar projects in similar settings. They want evaluators (both internal and external) to maintain an objective viewpoint while demonstrating an understanding of their client's organizational work environments and a sensitivity to the clients' needs for information. Recommendations for action are also expected from evaluators. Whereas upper-level administrators want evaluators to collect and present information in a standard manner, for ease of interpretation, individuals in smaller units of organizations often want evaluators to detect uniqueness and distinctiveness. Clients want short, concise reports that they can clearly understand. Evaluation reports must be free of unfamiliar language and jargon. Reports must include information that is perceived as credible by the client, that is, information from trustworthy sources. Finally, evaluators must complete their reports on time.

We have found that our work's usefulness can be enhanced if we plan evaluation activities that address the expectations of our clients. Unfortunately, we often work for more than one client at a time, and unresolvable conflicts may exist because multiple clients demonstrate different and often opposing needs for information.

When we serve as external evaluators, such conflicts seem less severe to us, because our clients are more explicitly identified. When we work as internal evaluators, however, the issue is more complex, as we simultaneously report to several clients. Even though we formally report to a central office, our long-term success on campus depends on our acceptance by several audiences and on our ability to meet the multiple expectations. Those who hire us expect us to be professional but also to act in a responsive and responsible manner consistent with organizational goals and procedures. Assuming no organizational responsibility is not an option, in our view.

Reference

Braskamp, L. A., Brandenburg, D. C., and Ory, J. C. *Evaluating Teaching Effectiveness: A Practical Guide.* Newbury Park, Calif.: Sage, 1984.

Larry A. Braskamp is currently associate vice-chancellor for academic affairs at the University of Illinois at Urbana-Champaign. He was a member of the University of Nebraska, Lincoln, faculty and served as assistant to the chancellor. At the University of Illinois, he was previously head of the Measurement and Research Division and acting director of the Executive Development Center.

Dale C. Brandenburg is currently associate head of the Division of Measurement and Evaluation, Office of Instructional and Management Services, at the University of Illinois at Urbana-Champaign. He holds an M.A. in educational psychology from Michigan State University and a Ph.D. in educational measurement from the University of Iowa. He was codesigner of the Instructor and Course Evaluation System (ICES), the student rating instrument used at UIUC and other institutions.

John C. Ory is currently head of the Division of Measurement and Evaluation at the University of Illinois at Urbana-Champaign. He holds M.A. and Ph.D. degrees in educational psychology from the University of Kansas. As an associate professor in the Department of Educational Psychology, he received the department's Outstanding Teaching Award in 1983.

A collaboration based on shared understanding characterizes
the client-evaluator relationship in this evaluation of a Roman
Catholic religious congregation.

Shared Understanding
of Organizational Culture

Thomas P. Faase, Steve Pujdak

The religious group that was evaluated is a nationwide province of a worldwide congregation. There are sixteen major "houses" of the province in the United States. They are widely disparate. About a third of the membership lives separately from any of these houses. The province also has mission assignments in Africa. The total membership of the province at the time of the evaluation was 205 members.

The main purpose of an upcoming provincial chapter (meeting) was to deliberate and make decisions regarding the "consolidation of apostolates." This would entail retrenchment of the works of the province, due to decreasing membership. The issue that the client faced was the following: If the administration retrenched by closing down and eliminating some of the geographical sites occupied by members of the province, would the membership be more likely to comply, or might they leave the congregation entirely? The client's question was this: What would be the implications for the province of the occurrence and timing of this retrenchment?

Retrenchment had been rumored by the rank-and-file members for two years. Views, feelings, and projections were mixed among the membership; resistance to dealing with the matter was widespread. Time was a constraint for the evaluation. The province chapter already scheduled

J. Nowakowski (ed.). *The Client Perspective on Evaluation.*
New Directions for Program Evaluation, no. 36. San Francisco: Jossey-Bass, Winter 1987.

allowed no more than six months from the time the evaluation commenced to the time the final report was to be distributed.

Selection of the Evaluator

The client wanted a consultant knowledgeable about the sociology of religion and about research in religious settings. He believed life in religious congregations is different enough from other forms of organizational participation to make the religious context indecipherable to the traditionally trained organizational analyst.

From the client's perspective, the selection of an evaluator was critical. Against a backdrop of previous research that had proved inadequate, the decision to proceed with another researcher had to be a tested judgment. The provincial chapter would occur with or without a research report. The report had been promised, and the chapter was planned around it, but there were misgivings that the issues were too weighty and sensitive to be represented in an evaluation research study. In the mind of the client, the decision to accept the researcher and to proceed with the evaluation research had to be a tiered decision. Two factors held sway: The time constraint was a real one, and there was a conviction that no evaluation report would be preferable to an inadequate one.

A sequence of go/no-go steps was involved. First of all, an assurance of the ability to meet the severe time constraints was required. This requirement was satisfied by a tight time schedule detailed in the evaluation research proposal. Second, there was the requirement to probe for an answer to the question "Why?" This requirement led to an explanatory evaluation research design selected in conference with the entire planning team of the province. Third, there was the problem of whether to confront the rank-and-file members with an explicit inquiry about retrenchment. This problem ultimately was resolved as progressive contact between client and evaluator brought assurances that important sensitivities could and would be honored in contacts with these stakeholders. The evaluation could not have begun without shared understanding and trust.

As the plan of evaluation and what could realistically be expected continued to unfold, it became increasingly clear that an evaluation could be done that would focus on questions critical to undertaking "consolidation, change, and expansion" of apostolates, and done in the depth required. In addition, the time constraint could be dealt with, although it would mean tight scheduling. Commitment to the project was finally made.

The Client-Evaluator Relationship

The client-evaluator relationship can be analyzed usefully to explain the importance of a shared understanding of organizational culture. Throughout the process, the client was substantively in control but needed to be procedurally counseled. For example, the client knew the organization and what was wanted from its members, but the evaluator suggested how to go about getting desired information. From the beginning, the client sensed the kinds of factors, dilemmas, difficulties, and so forth that the membership was beset by. Furthermore, the client was able to explicitly state these to the evaluator.

The evaluator offered possibilities to address these elements and offered options. The shape of the evaluation research came to light. It became apparent to the evaluator and to the client that they should study organizational and cultural variables more than individual variables, and that the evaluator was able to enter into and understand the uniqueness of the religious community without thereby shedding the "outsider" perspective and "objectivity" he was expected to bring to the project.

Interactive Preparation of the Design

Tailoring the design and, later, the instruments for data collection was accomplished through collaboration and interaction. Once the evaluator and the client recognized that they shared important religious understanding, there still remained the problem of different terminology. The evaluator had his, the client had his. They had to translate for each other on many occasions.

The technical language and process of evaluation research was shared through a working paper in preparation of a design, which was accompanied by schematic drawings of steps of the process. The working paper was presented to a planning team and began with informal lessons in evaluational research and step-by-step mapping of considerations, options, and decisions.

The value of this working paper was threefold. First, it allowed planning of the evaluation to proceed on the basis of well-informed judgment, with continual clarification of technical matters. Those who were involved as planners or other consultants during this phase of the evaluation never had the sense of being "snowed." Second, the idiosyncrasies and sensitivities of the province could be attended to through the strategies for inquiry. Third, the time devoted to the collaboration process heightened the investment of all concerned and strongly fostered the province's appropriation of the evaluation as its own.

The degree of client involvement in these stages may come as a surprise to some and may even appear to compromise the objectivity for which an evaluator is engaged. We submit, however, that such involvement contributed to rather than detracted from the thoroughness and comprehensibility of the evaluator's objective stance.

Instrument Construction

Shared understanding of the client's organizational culture provided a medium for item and instrument construction. The first draft of the instrument was done independently by the evaluator. Revision and finalization were done in collaboration with the client. The biggest part of the job was finding the right terminology. The language of the questionnaires had to reflect the idiosyncratic use of language of the province. This was accomplished by almost a reversal of what had happened in the design process.

In the design process, the client told the evaluator what he wanted, and the evaluator outlined procedures that might bring it about. In questionnaire construction, the evaluator told the client what he was trying to do, and the client helped arrive at the expression of it that would be best understood by the rank-and-file membership.

The evaluator knew the kinds of questions to ask, the ones that would yield information that could be analyzed and be useful to the client. In this instance, the evaluator's familiarity with the value systems of church groups and religious communities provided an indispensable background and framework within which to ask appropriate questions. Even with that advantage, however, the client had greater familiarity with this particular group; he knew who would respond to the question and how they might react to the choice of a word or a twist of a phrase.

The evaluator had the substance, and the client knew the idiosyncrasies. For this reason, evaluator and client worked together to hammer out the implications of every question and made sure that what was being asked was within the conceptual framework the evaluator had presented and the client had accepted. This translation and delimitation was a thoroughgoing negotiation. Five to six hours of planning and subsequent review, for instance, went into the construction of a single item on one scale.

Eliciting Administrative and Provincial Support

The close collaboration between client and evaluator had the effect of eliciting strong administrative support from the leaders of the province for every phase of the research. The chief executive of the province signed the introductory letter to the membership, advising them of the forthcoming survey and urging their participation. The final response rate was 90 percent of the membership.

Again, the way things happen in evaluation cannot always be accounted for rationally. Previous experience had made the membership wary and uncooperative. There was real resistance to the issues presented by the evaluation. The high rate of participation in this project and the cooperation of administrators and rank-and-file members were surprising and gratifying.

In a religious congregation, the rumor mill informs people about what is going on well before it happens. In this project, rumors assisted participation and the response rate. The collaboration of client and evaluator became evident in the early stages of the project. The planners who worked through the formulation of the research design were flown in from various places around the country to give input to the evaluation. Word spread that the evaluation under way was grounded in and well attuned to the concerns of the membership. The lesson from this is not new. Shared understanding affected the evaluation covertly, at least as much as in more obvious ways.

The Analysis Phase

Most interaction ended for a time, when the evaluator set out to do the analysis; the integrity of the data and the confidentiality that had been promised to the respondents excluded the client from this phase. Furthermore, the technical nature of the analysis made it the evaluator's responsibility. The effects of collaboration and shared understanding were exerted in the analysis phase indirectly, through the influence of the research design.

Results and Recommendations

The report of findings was a three-stage process. First, a preliminary report was made to the province staff by the evaluator. Next, a final report was sent out to the entire membership of the province one month before the chapter. Finally, the evaluator presented the findings to the chapter delegates in the context of the retrenchment deliberations.

The first report was preliminary. It was made to the provincial staff midway through the analysis. It showed the direction of responses. It permitted the staff to put questions to the evaluator for additional or subsequent analysis. Some issues received new emphasis and were thereby treated more explicitly in the final written report. The preliminary report had another function for the staff: It calmed some fears on the part of staff people who were involved in planning the chapter.

The second part of the three-stage presentation of findings was writing the final report. This was unusual in that the client participated actively in a pervasive revision of a first draft of the report. To the client, it was not a matter of changing the substance of the report, but rather of reviewing it for clarity. If a sentence or a paragraph was ambiguous, would this be perceived as design or accident? Once again, choice of word and turns of phrase were carefully scrutinized, and they were revised only when the evaluator was convinced that changes would make a difference in communication. In all cases of suggested revisions, the evaluator held the veto over any change. Some interpretations were challenged by the client. Of these, most remained, but with clarification. On a more pragmatic level, the client brought to the writing fine editorial and clarifying skills. More than a few flourishes were eliminated, and some inconsistencies were obviated.

A definite strength of the report was that it was prepared for the entire membership of the province, after 90 percent of the membership had responded to the sensitive inquiry. Candid and relevant information was conveyed with the sense that it would have impact on everyone concerned. As it turned out, the major recommendations went contrary to plans for retrenchment and to the sense of urgency felt about retrenchment by most of the administrative staff.

The third stage of presentation took place at the chapter itself. One-tenth of the province membership participated. The evaluation came to the assembly in a dialectic with another report that had been written by a member of the province staff prior to and irrespective of the evaluation. Side by side, the two reports formed a striking contrast: The insider document said that consolidation and retrenchment should wait no longer. The evaluation recommended that retrenchment be delayed and said that its implementation would be premature. An outside facilitator was used to chair the sessions dealing with the issues raised in both reports. The procedure resembled an advocacy-adversary form of evaluation.

The reception of the oral presentation of the evaluation results and recommendations evidenced an extension of the "chemistry" that had gone into the collaboration of client and researcher. The report had a compelling presence in the chapter due to shared understanding.

The decision taken at the chapter was to accept the recommendations and implement a program that delayed retrenchment, while instigating more activity and deliberation among rank-and-file members. The program would prepare members more directly for retrenchment, elicit greater ownership of the issues, procedures, and priorities, and occasion greater cultural allegiance among the membership.

Reflections by the Evaluator

From the point of view of the evaluator, collaboration was both the easiest and the most difficult way to do evaluation. It was easiest because it did not demand feigned expertise, role playing, or bearing of the whole burden of the enterprise. The entire project was shaped interactively. The strengths of the evaluation came from an array of needs and cues about the client that emerged out of many conversations. Tailor-making the evaluation research design built confidence. Relevance seemed ensured. The insights that mattered most at the time of the analysis had been "collected" throughout the project. The movement of thought to assertion stemming from the analysis and leading to recommendations was made possible by much of what had happened in the previous collaboration. By the time of the final report, the evaluator felt like a seasoned veteran in the conditions of the client. Furthermore, something enlivening and gratifying in the "chemistry" that developed between client and evaluator fueled a passion for the success of the project, which left its mark on the final written report and on the report to the chapter.

Collaboration was also the most difficult way to do evaluation. It demanded a great deal of time. With the constraints of the overall schedule, it entailed long hours of many days and far exceeded the number of hours projected when the proposal was first submitted. It was difficult to work with a wide array of personnel and try to reconcile the needs of all of them. Every step of the process was amended at least once.

What was most difficult of all (and, in an ironic way, also most gratifying), the evaluator assumed the stance of a peer, rather than that of a specialized professional. It would have been easier to rest on protocol than to be exposed in tentativeness. The evaluator would have "looked better" bringing in a printed version of a survey instrument than showing the cut-and-paste version of the last draft of that instrument. The evaluator would have seemed so much more competent handing in a word-processed and spiral-bound final report instead of coming in with packs of handwritten pages, with revisions and corrections penciled in and ready to undergo the awful scrutiny of the client's editorial expertise. The evaluator was vulnerable in such situations. At times, in fact, when uncertainty about how the whole project would "fly" with the chapter came over both evaluator and client like a dark cloud, the suspense and self-doubt became palpable. The answer at these moments was not to compromise the report but to mutually support the clarity and quality of what both parties believed had been done well.

Reflections by the Client

Any evaluator who intends to meet the needs of a client has to be carefully attuned to the uniqueness of the client's particular group. For example, different segments of society can benefit from insights drawn from the corporate model, but wholesale transposition of one environment to another, without necessary and appropriate adjustment, ill serves any client. While this might appear to have greater relevance for religious communities and their belief systems, similar claims can be made for academic environments, social action groups, and so forth. An evaluator who shares the basic values of the client can more readily see the issues and more clearly address them.

The client should work closely with the evaluator in as many facets of evaluation as possible. It is not enough to outline one's concerns and then sit back to await the final report. The evaluator should help the client formulate the focus, but the client has to be sure that the questions are his own and that they address his own issues. The more the client understands and can take ownership for what went into the "front end" of the project, the more likely it is that he will comprehend and accept the results.

Thomas P. Faase is associate professor of sociology at St. Norbert College in DePere, Wisconsin. He specializes in a sociology of human values, and his research has dealt with change in and evaluation of religious groups and congregations.

Steve Pujdak is a priest of the Congregation of the Sacred Heart. After doctoral studies in Louvain and teaching at Marquette University, he became planning director of the S.C.J. province and now serves as provincial secretary.

The Illinois State director of research and evaluation discusses issues related to commissioning and using evaluation.

Evaluation Research in State-Level Decision Making

Interview with Sally B. Pancrazio by Patricia F. First

First: Sally, you only recently were appointed to the new position of chief of research and program evaluation for the Illinois State Board of Education [ISBE] but you have spent many years managing the evaluation research issues we will discuss. How long have you been with the ISBE as manager of research and statistics?

Pancrazio: I've been manager for over thirteen years, but the functions of the position have changed over time.

F: We are going to discuss your work from the client's perspective. In thinking of your office as client, we might group providers of evaluation and research data into three categories: in-house staff; contractees, such as professors; and the field, that is, the local education agencies [LEAs], the cooperatives, and the regional entities that report to your office. How do you use each of these groups, Sally?

P: First, the staff primarily prepare research reports to facilitate decision making and/or policy making. Sometimes reports are merely descriptive and don't have specific, direct policy relevance. Our early reports, twelve years ago or so, were all descriptive. Now, however, our reports have become increasingly policy-relevant as top management has

J. Nowakowski (ed.). *The Client Perspective on Evaluation.*
New Directions for Program Evaluation, no. 36. San Francisco: Jossey-Bass, Winter 1987.

recognized the need to move in that direction. The staff primarily prepares or conducts research that will assist top management, the state superintendent, and our state board in decision making and/or policy development.

F: And when do you use contracts?

P: Studies which are contracted out are designed to meet specific needs and those needs are varied. They have a commonality in one way. They represent work that we are unable to perform within the agency. Either the timelines are too short, staff are not available to do the work, or the expertise and knowledge to do the work are not present on our staff, specifically the research section.

F: How do you use the field?

P: We collect data from the field that the state board of education has indicated are necessary for public reporting, such as basic statistical information on the condition of Illinois education, or representative data like one-time-only assessments of attitudes or reactions.

F: If you use each type of group for somewhat different needs, is the kind of research that you ask them to do also different?

P: Yes. The kinds of research staff do vary significantly and include reviews of the literature, qualitative issues analysis, synthesis of research findings, descriptive study, analysis of statistical data involving sophisticated procedures for testing the presence of relevant relationships, projection of data, such as an enrollment projection, or an opinion or needs assessment. School finance researchers also conduct research that simulates prospective changes in a state aid formula so that we can predict impact.

We don't do laboratory or highly controlled research, such as research involving interaction between teacher and learner, although we may assess from students and teachers what their achievement happens to be or we might collect information about the achievement. That doesn't mean that controlled studies aren't sometimes mandated by the legislature. In fact, there are two studies being conducted now which relate to the effectiveness of early childhood programs for at-risk children as well as young handicapped children. Both of these require an experimental or quasi-experimental design. For these two studies, we will contract with others outside the agency. Again, I turn to contractors where we don't have the expertise or the time. Because of our mission, we are not likely to conduct the kind of controlled design required in an experimental or quasi-experimental study.

F: Tell us something about your staff, about the nature of their expertise. My impression is that your staff is large and comprehensive, but how does it compare with other state agencies?

P: There are twenty professional staff. The majority are people who have or soon will have a doctorate. They primarily received their research training in the experimental mode, and most of them then acquired descriptive research skills and survey skills as a result of working in the agency. All of them have skills in synthesizing and reviewing literature.

F: And do staff have educational specialties?

P: Yes, although in the past several years, we have attempted to hire more "generic" researchers—people with computer backgrounds and good analysis and writing skills. Earlier, however, we hired people who had expertise in school finance, curriculum, or teacher education. We are moving toward the generic because the varied types of demands made on us don't lend themselves to such specificity.

F: How do you guide design decisions when dealing with staff, consultants, and field evaluators?

P: The design depends first on the purpose for conducting the study, second on how much time we have, and third on how much error we can permit in the study. As you are well aware, policymakers will make decisions on whatever information they have at the time they need to make the decision. So we have to take into account their information needs, the calendars of our board and the legislature, and whatever else is happening in terms of the timing. It is very different from university or laboratory research, I think, in that we are very sensitive to the time in which we conduct the study, the time in which it has to be completed, and the time when information is to be released. All those constitute possibly sensitive factors, about which other kind of researchers may not have to be concerned.

F: Then timeliness is a major design concern across all information providers. Are there other design concerns?

P: Timeliness is a problem across all groups, but with staff, there is another problem. Because they are researchers employed within the state organization, there is a built-in caution about generalizing from their studies. They may have better information than anybody else has, but some are very cautious and reluctant to assess a policy implication from the data. I don't think they want to be responsible for the action taken by policymakers.

F: Do you think it goes back to that traditional research training?

P: Yes. They are trained to look for the limits in research and its problems, as opposed to recognizing that policymakers make decisions based on whatever information they have, almost regardless of its foundation. So although our researchers may have the best information available, they are by training and by nature reluctant to say, "This is what it means" or "This is what it does not mean." And that's one of the frustrations: getting people to generalize and search for implications. It's very difficult.

F: Do you often find that their caution puts you personally in the role of generating the policy implications?

P: Yes, and in many ways it is a management prerogative, but it would be helpful if the researchers could free themselves from their early training and be more a James Coleman-type researcher—not afraid of the implications of their research. Coleman's work has been controversial, true, but he has stimulated people's conversations and thinking and dialogue about educational problems in a way that many other researchers never do. He gets criticized for that. On the other hand, his research is also known to many people outside of education, and most educational research is not.

F: Do you see ways for the staff to free themselves from these restrictions?

P: A manager can encourage and build in more opportunities. There has to be a balance. You don't want researchers to become advocates, or else they lose their unique function as researchers, but I am more worried about them moving toward the center than going off on the radical end. In terms of contractors—with, actually, two exceptions— most research that we have contracted out over the years has been very disappointing to us, because it is so highly technical and lacks utility. Even the titles of the papers generally suggest methodology, rather than use. For example, "The Multiple-Regression Analysis of Thus and So" emphasizes the statistical technique used, as opposed to the usefulness of the findings.

F: Do these kinds of research reports all come from professors, or are there also other providing groups?

P: They've all been professors, and even the best of them—again, with two exceptions—have fallen into this "methodology trap." It may be that they just don't understand state education agencies, or perhaps it's another symptom of the cautious researcher.

F: Perhaps they have a perception that this is what state agencies want, and they can't get beyond that.

P: That's a good observation. We are not a research agency that is designed to work 100 percent of our time in providing information services or expanding knowledge. That's nice if we could do it, and we do try to do it to some extent, but our primary clientele is the state superintendent, the state board, and other groups that they designate. Professors' terminology just doesn't lend itself toward the kinds of people who read government reports, so we've had to rewrite them, reformat them, and again emphasize the usefulness of the findings, as opposed to the methodology.

F: Do other sections in the state agency look to your research section for guidance in design, in how to deal with contractors?

P: Yes, they do, and we call it providing technical assistance to others. What we find, and this is a constant problem, is that they want us to dictate what they ought to make of this information; they want us to make departmental decisions. Our staff say, "Tell me what you want, or tell me what you need," and they say, "Well, we don't know what we want. Why don't you tell us what our options are, and then we can say yes or no to them." It gets very frustrating for my staff.

F: How do you compare research groups in other state agencies to yours?

P: Illinois is mandated by law to have a research department. All state agencies have statistical units, but not all have research staff or functions. Depending on the state, they may have staff who work with public relations or with publications. There may be a research-type person who writes speeches for the state superintendent and also does an occasional research synthesis, that kind of thing. But most of the large state agencies do have both research and evaluation staff. An AERA SIG group for state education agency staff is still in operation after thirteen or fourteen years.

F: Sally, in studying a big issue, such as educational reform, which is happening all across the states and is happening in a big way in Illinois, do you find that you and your research staff are comparing what you are doing with other states, so that there will be some sort of comprehensive measures of reform?

P: I think that one of the major questions that we are always asked by state policymakers is "How does Illinois compare with other states, particularly the big industrial states like New York, Pennsylvania, California, and Michigan, and with the nation in general?" And so we do try to keep up on similar types of requirements. For example, as a result of national assessment, expertise in assessment programs has developed in many state agencies. In terms of evaluating each specific reform, I think program managers would check with a group like the Education Commission of the States, the National Association of State Legislatures, the National Association of State Boards of Education, or the Council of Chief State School Officers to find out what other states are doing. It's just been in the last five or six years, at least in Illinois, that the importance of linking research with policy has not only become overt but is encouraged. As a result of understanding the importance of information to policy development and evaluation, we have become staff to the state superintendent's office for that very purpose.

F: Can you see a difference in the quality of information used to make policy decisions today? Can you see research making more of a difference?

P: Yes, I see it in the quality of the discussions that occur. That is one measure. Another measure is that none of our policy reports—for example, the more than a dozen studies conducted from 1981 to 1985 in preparation for educational reform—was attacked on the basis of the research design and findings.

F: That must have made you feel proud.

P: It did, of course, but I was only one of many staff involved. The research process as part of policy development and evaluation was in place, so that compiling, gathering, analyzing, and then debating educationally sound policy alternatives was possible. Educational soundness was the first criterion used. The feasibility and political acceptability of policy alternatives were also criteria, but they were not criteria used by our staff. They were used by the state board of education once it began its policy deliberations. We were directed not to make political or fiscal decisions and not to let those two factors in any way shape the research aspect. This freed policymakers to discuss each recommendation on the basis of its merits. Although not all of our recommendations were enacted into legislation, most of them were.

F: My own dissertation study found that premature consideration of monetary or legal problems killed policy options. It's good to hear that staff have been freed from those restrictions and can take some creative options back to their client—the state board.

P: It was difficult for us to get out of that model and not balk when a proposal, such as full-day kindergarten, was going to cost millions and millions of dollars. Once staff are freed of those constraints, it is amazing what can come forth. Considering policy *before* finance at least allows a policy consideration on the agenda, and it is considered and debated on a healthy, sound basis, rather than with a bias that no one is going to accept it fiscally, so why advance it.

F: Sometimes LEAs [local education agencies] complain of having to report so much evaluation information to the state board, and they don't necessarily know how it is used or even whether it is used. How would you respond to them?

P: I would agree with them. We are very sensitive to the response burden on local school districts. They have been burdened by data requests throughout the years, not only by the state but also by the feds and other types of researchers. As you know, our own board has set up a practice whereby we have to justify every new information element that we gather from LEAs. This does limit what we collect, but every element has been demonstrated to have specific use. It's our job to communicate that to the LEAs. We don't always do that as best we can.

F: Are LEAs becoming aware of this requirement through the different State Board advisory boards on which they have seats?

P: I think so. I think that it is a truism that we are becoming an information society, that more and more people are asking better and better questions, that more people want evidence to show what works or to describe the status of education. Even among the power groups there exists the recognition that information is needed to improve the quality of the debate about an issue. From LEAs, again, our biggest frustration is getting information back on time.

F: Ah, timeliness! I was going to guess quality control.

P: Quality control is a secondary issue, because we have set up computer, logical, and manual edit checks to enhance the probability that we get accurate data from LEA providers. We are also moving toward electronic data transmission, which increases the likelihood of collecting accurate data because they can't be entered unless done so properly. But timeliness is still a problem. The more sophisticated a school district is, however, the less the problem. The larger districts are probably better equipped to collect, aggregate, and report evaluation data than are districts of three hundred or four hundred or fewer students.

F: Can you speak to the evaluation research problems inherent in the fact that we have one thousand school districts?

P: It's a real problem because of the quality-control issue. In small districts, the superintendent does everything, or a clerical person will be providing very important information and not necessarily recognizing its importance.

F: The Illinois report card is a district profile used for self-assessment and district comparisons. Most of the data are generated from test scores and attendance and graduation records. Tell us about the development of the report cards and how they are working out as an evaluation strategy.

P: The school report card is a requirement, made of all Illinois public schools, to report certain kinds of information annually, no later than October 31 of every year, beginning in 1986. This is a new requirement in the Education Reform Act, and it was supported by legislators and the governor as an accountability measure. The school report card was seen as a mechanism by which taxpayers, business people, community, and parents would have information they would need in order to assess how well the schools were doing. It was recognized that this was not a diagnostic tool for individual children, but rather a uniform way of reporting the same information across all schools. As you know, it was very controversial. District superintendents were very negative about the report card and very vocal about how damaging such information would be to their public relations, their community, to property values, to teachers, to principals, and to kids and parents. They said it would rip Illinois education apart. There were fourteen other states that had similar, though not identical, requirements. None of that happened in any of the other states, and I was sure it wouldn't happen here. But administrators were afraid of the public finding out certain information about schools and then having the capacity to compare information across schools and school districts. They were very much afraid of the comparisons.

F: How did you actually develop the format, then, given all of this turmoil?

P: We just plowed ahead on what needed to be done. We also had considerable support from such community groups as the Farm Bureau, the State Chamber of Commerce, and the Taxpayers' Federation.

F: Did the superintendents see the report card, in the end, as a vehicle for reporting both strengths and weaknesses of their districts?

P: The attitudes they indicated changed significantly. A survey showed that we had an increased number who said that after going through it, they were much more positive about the report card. We still had 20 percent who, both before and after, held very negative attitudes about the requirement. I think what the report card did was showcase a lot of school districts. Throughout September and October, there was article after article about the schools in the newspapers, most very positive. I think the report card's value is that it provides an opportunity to raise questions about the schools, and this in itself was healthy for the Illinois public. People read the cards, and it led to asking questions about why one school was so different from another school, or why it wasn't different from another school, and that spirit of inquiry and questioning can only be healthy for Illinois education. I really believe that we will see more of that inquiry and healthy questioning as we become more sophisticated in displaying this information.

F: What do you see coming down the pike that might be different in the way your division operates, now that you are chief of evaluation as well as research and statistics?

P: That's a good question. We will become more involved in evaluating the administration of policy and programs. That will be a change from working with administration to evaluate other aspects of programs. Most of our present reports are descriptive; they answer the basic questions about how many students are being served, the demographics of the students, program cost, and kinds of services being provided. But they don't answer value questions, such as "Does the program do what it was designed to do? Does it do it well? Does it do it poorly? How can it be improved? Are there policies or rules and laws that prevent children from getting these services? Are there other ways to meet the objectives? Are children encountering barriers to good education?" We'll be looking at those kinds of value issues, with an emphasis on children and the quality of services they receive and the importance of those children becoming educated and well-informed citizens.

F: Any final words about designing evaluations so that they contribute to state policy making, such as those described?

P: I notice that many federal policy studies come from a major federal data collection, such as High School and Beyond. They are very good, technically excellent, and very useful data bases. One strategy that we have used at the state level, however, is that when we do policy studies, we don't rely on one data set or one data base. We look at the problem from a variety of data bases. We conduct a good literature review, and then we often combine it with some descriptive study of what the current status in Illinois is on this particular issue. The resulting policy study uses multiple data bases and has very rich content, as opposed to being restricted by an initial set of variables probably selected years before. I would recommend that the field not limit itself to one data base in the development of policy studies.

A second recommendation is that there should be a differentiation by policy researchers about the level of policy making. Is it to be at the federal level? The state level? Each focus requires a little different strategy in conducting a study; although the study components may be the same, the way you use them is different. I think there has to be a recognition that certain strategies may be appropriate for study at one level and not for another. And part of that is learning that design of an evaluation study is an art form, in many ways.

My third recommendation is to recognize that there are beliefs to ignore, such as "You never have as much information as you want" and "You never have it when you want it." Policymakers are going to make decisions on incomplete information, and it is far better to have timely information than it is to have perfect information. Obviously, you want accurate information, but the cost of getting that over meeting timelines is too high. If we have to sacrifice one for the other, we say that findings are "preliminary" or data are "estimates." We make information available when people need to make decisions, because we know they will not wait.

Sally B. Pancrazio is chief of research and program evaluation at the Illinois State Board of Education, where she has managed research functions for over thirteen years. She is also adjunct professor of educational research at Illinois State University and has authored numerous articles on management topics.

Patricia F. First is chair of the faculty in educational administration and school business management at Northern Illinois University, where she specializes in policy analysis and the politics of education. She was previously a planning/policy analyst with the Illinois State Board of Education.

Index

U.S. POSTAL SERVICE
STATEMENT OF OWNERSHIP, MANAGEMENT AND CIRCULATION
(Required by 39 U.S.C. 3685)

1. TITLE OF PUBLICATION	A. PUBLICATION NO.	2. DATE OF FILING
New Directions for Program Evaluation	4 4 9 - 0 5 0	10/7/87

3. FREQUENCY OF ISSUE	A. NO. OF ISSUES PUBLISHED ANNUALLY	B. ANNUAL SUBSCRIPTION PRICE
quarterly	4	$39 indiv/$52 inst

4. COMPLETE MAILING ADDRESS OF KNOWN OFFICE OF PUBLICATION *(Street, City, County, State and ZIP Code) (Not printers)*
433 California St., San Francisco, San Francisco County, CA 94104

5. COMPLETE MAILING ADDRESS OF THE HEADQUARTERS OR GENERAL BUSINESS OFFICES OF THE PUBLISHERS *(Not printers)*
433 California St., San Francisco, San Francisco County, CA 94104

6. FULL NAMES AND COMPLETE MAILING ADDRESS OF PUBLISHER, EDITOR, AND MANAGING EDITOR *(This item MUST NOT be blank)*
PUBLISHER *(Name and Complete Mailing Address)*
Jossey-Bass Inc., Publishers, 433 California St., San Francisco CA 94104

EDITOR *(Name and Complete Mailing Address)*
Mark W. Lipsey, Psychology Dept., Claremont Grad School, Claremont CA 91711

MANAGING EDITOR *(Name and Complete Mailing Address)*
Allen Jossey-Bass, Jossey-Bass Publishers, 433 California St., SF CA 94104

7. OWNER *(If owned by a corporation, its name and address must be stated and also immediately thereunder the names and addresses of stockholders owning or holding 1 percent or more of total amount of stock. If not owned by a corporation, the names and addresses of the individual owners must be given. If owned by a partnership or other unincorporated firm, its name and address, as well as that of each individual must be given. If the publication is published by a nonprofit organization, its name and address must be stated.) (Item must be completed.)*

FULL NAME	COMPLETE MAILING ADDRESS
Jossey-Bass Inc., Publishers	433 California St., SF CA 94104

for names and addresses of stockholders, see attached list

8. KNOWN BONDHOLDERS, MORTGAGEES, AND OTHER SECURITY HOLDERS OWNING OR HOLDING 1 PERCENT OR MORE OF TOTAL AMOUNT OF BONDS, MORTGAGES OR OTHER SECURITIES *(If there are none, so state)*

FULL NAME	COMPLETE MAILING ADDRESS
same as #7	

9. FOR COMPLETION BY NONPROFIT ORGANIZATIONS AUTHORIZED TO MAIL AT SPECIAL RATES *(Section 411.3, DMM only)*
The purpose, function, and nonprofit status of this organization and the exempt status for Federal income tax purposes *(Check one)*

(1) ☐ HAS NOT CHANGED DURING PRECEDING 12 MONTHS
(2) ☐ HAS CHANGED DURING PRECEDING 12 MONTHS
(If changed, publisher must submit explanation of change with this statement.)

10. EXTENT AND NATURE OF CIRCULATION	AVERAGE NO. COPIES EACH ISSUE DURING PRECEDING 12 MONTHS	ACTUAL NO. COPIES OF SINGLE ISSUE PUBLISHED NEAREST TO FILING DATE
A. TOTAL NO. COPIES *(Net Press Run)*	3200	3412
B. PAID CIRCULATION 1. SALES THROUGH DEALERS AND CARRIERS, STREET VENDORS AND COUNTER SALES	92	46
2. MAIL SUBSCRIPTION	2804	2975
C. TOTAL PAID CIRCULATION *(Sum of 10B1 and 10B2)*	2896	3021
D. FREE DISTRIBUTION BY MAIL, CARRIER OR OTHER MEANS SAMPLES, COMPLIMENTARY, AND OTHER FREE COPIES	108	118
E. TOTAL DISTRIBUTION *(Sum of C and D)*	3004	3139
F. COPIES NOT DISTRIBUTED 1. OFFICE USE, LEFT OVER, UNACCOUNTED, SPOILED AFTER PRINTING	196	273
2. RETURN FROM NEWS AGENTS		
G. TOTAL *(Sum of E, F1 and 2 - should equal net press run shown in A)*	3200	3412

11. I certify that the statements made by me above are correct and complete
SIGNATURE AND TITLE OF EDITOR, PUBLISHER, BUSINESS MANAGER, OR OWNER
Vice-President

PS Form 3526, July 1981 *(See instruction on reverse)* *(Page 1)*